C000254960

ΘΕΟΣ

GOD, MAN,

THE BIBLE

& LIFE

ΠΙΣΤΙΣ

The Costa Rica Conference Lectures

STEVEN R. MARTINS

To my dear friend and brother in the faith,
Julian Castaño, who proved to be a Barnabas with a
Pauline spirit on our ministry journey together.

~ Steven R. Martins

cántaro
publications

www.cantaroinstitute.org

Published by Cántaro Publications, a publishing imprint of the Cántaro Institute, Jordan Station, ON.

Book design by Steven R. Martins

Library & Archives Canada

ISBN 978-1-9990992-9-9

About the Cántaro Institute
Inheriting, Informing, Inspiring

The Cántaro Institute is a confessional evangelical Christian organization established in 2020 that seeks to recover the riches of Spanish Protestantism for the renewal and edification of the contemporary church and to advance the comprehensive Christian philosophy of life for the religious reformation of the Western and Ibero-American world.

We believe that as the Christian church returns to the fount of Scripture as her ultimate authority for all knowing and living, and wisely applies God's truth to every aspect of life, faithful in spirit to the reformers, her missiological activity will result in not only the renewal of the human person but also the reformation of culture, an inevitable result when the true scope and nature of the gospel is made known and applied.

This series of lectures, which I had the privilege to attend, exhibited the most consistent Van Tillian apologetic I have ever witnessed in Costa Rica, they provided an irrefutable defense of the Christian faith as the only worldview capable of making rational sense of reality. The ultimate statement that the proof of the Christian worldview lies in the impossibility of the contrary is a robust Van Tillian apologetic that has silenced many skeptics, leaving them without a foundation to stand on. I could see for myself that those who attended these lectures had a lot to chew on and digest.

—**Randolph H. Sperger**
International Director of the Iberoamerican
Fraternity of Frontier Missions, Costa Rica

*Organization representatives of Editorial CLIR and
Diálogos CIV with the founding directors of the Cántaro Institute
(Steven R. Martins, Julian Castaño, and Daniel J. Lobo)
in San Jose, Costa Rica*

Table of Contents

Editor's Note

God, Man, the Bible & Life is a collection of lectures delivered by the founding director of the Cántaro Institute, Steven R. Martins, during his visit to Costa Rica in 2017 for a multi-day apologetics conference organized by the reformed publishing house Editorial CLIR and the Christian academic thinktank Diálogos CIV. The lectures were delivered at the Biblioteca Luis Demetrio Tinoco of the Universidad de Costa Rica (UCR) and the Biblioteca Joaquín García Monge of the Universidad Nacional de Costa Rica (UNCR).

Speaking to a mixed audience of Christians, religious pluralists, skeptics and inquirers, Steven delivered four lectures relating to the truthfulness of the Christian worldview. In the first, so as to provide an epistemological foundation, he addressed the truthfulness and trustworthiness of the Bible. In the second, building on the foundation of the first, he addressed the uniqueness of Jesus and the exclusivity of his truth claims in an era of religious pluralism. In the third, he responded to the age-old question Can man live without God? And in the fourth, he concluded by addressing the ever relevant problem of evil.

Altogether, this collection of lectures, which are here published as they were originally given, serves to provide a defense for a distinctly biblical worldview, to equip and strengthen the faith of Christian readership, and to critically engage with skeptics and inquirers. In addition to these lectures, a conference paper that was also submitted for publishing is included, entitled The Muslim & Christian Mind, which addresses the subject of epistemology as it relates to the Islamic and Christian doctrines of God and man.

It is our hope that this book, in spite of the drawbacks that often come with publishing in this lecture form, inspires Christian readership to dig deeper into the comprehensive nature of their faith and to vehemently defend the true Christian philosophy of life. We also hope and anticipate that this publication challenges skeptics and inquirers to seriously question their presuppositions and to consider the true presuppositions of God's revealed word, that they might find all the answers to their heart's questions in the truth of the Christian worldview.

May God alone be glorified, *Soli Deo Gloria*

The Editorial Team
Cántaro Publications

The Trustworthiness of Scripture

"All Scripture is breathed out by God and profitable for teaching, for reproof, for correction, and for training in righteousness."

– 2 Timothy 3:16

1.1 Introduction

IN HONOUR OF THE 500ᵀᴴ anniversary of the protestant reformation, I believe it is fitting to open with the following words by Martin Luther – the German reformer of the 16th century – in relation to the Bible and its truthfulness:

> The Bible is the proper book for men. There the truth is distinguished from error far more clearly than anywhere else, and one finds something new in it every day. For twenty-eight years, since I became a scholar, I have now constantly read and preached the Bible; and yet I have not exhausted it but find something new in it every day.[1]

Five hundred years ago, the reformation began as

---

1. Martin Luther, *Weimarer Ausgabe Tischreden* 5, no. 5193.

an ecclesiological movement which sought to bring the church back to the singular authority of Scripture and the purity of the gospel. The Latin phrase that best expressed this principle was *Sola Scriptura* (Scripture alone). The other four *Solas* of Christian doctrine (*Sola Fide, Sola Gratia, Solus Christos,* and *Soli Deo Gloria*) were derived from this principal *Sola*.

On the occasion of initiating this multi-day conference, I had been asked to speak on the truthfulness and trustworthiness of the Bible. It is, in fact, a great privilege to speak on such a vital and relevant subject. However, from the start I must say that I am wholly *un*-apologetic for my position on the Christian Scriptures. As was the case for the reformers, it is likewise impossible for me, personally, to adopt a position of religious neutrality concerning the Bible. Like Luther, the Bible is the fount of my life and learning, it is the divinely inspired word of God unto all men, and I hope that by the end of this lecture, you too will recognize this sacred book as God's sovereign word-revelation. And if by God's providence you already do, then I trust and hope that this lecture will serve to further strengthen your faith in God's word.

To this day, the Bible has been on record as the most widely-distributed book in the world. Since the year 1815 (roughly when records were beginning to be regularly kept and preserved), more than 5 billion copies have been distributed in the West. It has been translated from its original Hebrew and Greek into *almost* all the known-languages of the world, and has reached every corner of the earth – even those countries in the

Middle-East, Asia, and other regions where it has been banned. It is a remarkable book like no other, and has left its mark on human civilization like no other book ever has.

In the Western world, the Bible was once revered and respected as the answer to the questions of our culture. As to the structure and direction of our society's institutions, whether they be the family, the church, the state, or the University, the Bible was generally the compass, map and guide. As it concerned the disciplines of academia – ranging from philosophy to the humanities – it made the study, development, and progress of the disciplines possible. And as it concerned justice and the right dignity of the human person, the Bible was the standard and point of reference. It was more than just a communication from God for mankind's spiritual salvation, it was the authoritative interpretation of reality, meant to be wisely applied to all areas of life, and informing us of God's promise for the restoration and renewal of the whole created order. But as the religious beliefs of the people changed over the course of time, the Bible became less an authority for mankind and more the subject of our culture's questions:

- How could the Bible have contributed towards the development of Western civilization?
- Can we trust the Bible's claim of infallibility and inerrancy?
- What does the Bible have to offer us and our present culture – if anything at all?

It is my earnest hope that I can provide satisfactory answers to these questions within such limited time by providing a (i) brief overview of the history and narrative of the Bible; (ii) its cultural contribution to the West; and (iii) the significance of the Bible's self-witness of its infallibility and inerrancy.

1.2 The History and Narrative of the Bible

To begin with, for those not familiar with the Bible's beginnings, the Bible came into being by the progressive revelation of God in human history, beginning first with the books of the Law of the Old Testament. The Old Testament is the result of Hebrew scribes, priests, prophets, kings and poets recording the history of their people – and this history consisting of their own covenant relationship with God. These writings were copied repeatedly from generation to generation, and were gathered into three collections: (1) the Law (*Torah*); (2) the Prophets (*Nevi'im*); and (3) the Writings (*Ketuvim*).

The *Torah* contained the first five books of the Bible, otherwise known as the Pentateuch (Genesis to Deuteronomy). The *Nevi'im* consisted of Isaiah, Jeremiah, Ezekiel, the Twelve Minor Prophets, Joshua, Judges, 1st and 2nd Samuel, and 1st and 2nd Kings. The *Ketuvim* included the rest of the Old Testament books, such as the great poetic books of the Psalms and Song of Solomon, the wisdom literature of Proverbs, Job, Ecclesiastes, and the books of Esther, Lamentations, Ruth, Daniel, Ezra, Nehemiah, and 1st and 2nd Chronicles. Some of these books have since been categorized under "Prophetic" and "Historical" books, but the Jews have traditionally maintained these three categories. These books altogether form the Hebrew Bible, or as referred to by Christians, the Old Testament.

What followed historically was the writing of the New Testament, and this consisted of the Gospels (the eye-witness accounts of Jesus), the Pauline epistles, pastoral letters, and the book of Revelation. These were written and circulated in the AD first century church, a community of Jesus-followers – both Hebrew and Gentile – in the same century and generation in which the recorded events had taken place. These books, together with the Old Testament, form the whole unity of the Christian Bible.

In spite of its diverse authorship, and its writings spanning 1,500 years, the Bible presents a single unified unfolding story: God's redemption of human beings and his promise to redeem the whole created order under His just governance. This just governance of God is often referred to by the Bible as the "Kingdom of God", and in other biblical passages "the Kingdom of Heaven." We find this kingdom theme beginning in the first book of the *Torah*, the book of Genesis. We can refer to this first instance as the **Pattern of the Kingdom**, in which the garden of Eden, created by God, serves as a reflection of the world as God designed it to be.[2] To elaborate: In the context of the first two chapters of Genesis, Adam and Eve are God's people (His creation), live in God's place (also His cre-

---

2. Vaughan Roberts, *God's Big Picture: Tracing the Storyline of the Bible* (Downers Grove, IL.: IVP Books, 2002), 24.

ation), and are under His kingly rule as they submit to God's law-word. The original state of creation as good, not fallen, was a reflection of what God's kingdom on earth was to be, with authority being delegated to man to cultivate God's creation into a godly civilization for the glory of God alone (Gen. 1:27-28).

But as outlined by biblical writer Vaughan Roberts, the **Pattern of the Kingdom** gave way to **Kingdom Lost**, as Adam and Eve sought complete independence from God[3] – this was, to put it plainly, man's pursuit to determine reality, ethics and knowledge for himself. Having rebelled against their Creator-King, they were no longer God's people. They remained His creation, but they were God's creatures in rebellion and hostility. They also forfeited their rightful claim and authority over creation (as had been given to them), and having disobeyed God's law-word, they were no longer under God's just governance (as they had initially desired), that is to say, no longer walking in obedience to God. The result of this rebellion was a curse which impacted not only the very core of man, that is to say, his being, but the whole of creation, which was under his dominion. Man would, ever since then, walk under the judgment of the Creator, experiencing the various ills of our fallen world.

The narrative of Scripture does not end in tragedy, however. In the third chapter of Genesis we find the promise of God concerning the restoration of His kingdom on earth and all things created (Gen. 3:15).

---

3. Ibid.

This **Promised Kingdom** will be realized through the descendants of Abraham, who will be God's people, living in the land that God will give them to govern, subject to His law-word.[4] This kingdom is only partially fulfilled through the nation of Israel in the Old Testament, and is therefore recognized as the **Partial Kingdom**, for as those who may be familiar with Old Testament history, Israel proved to be unfaithful to their God on multiple occasions.[5]

As a result of their continued and persistent infidelity, God had His people exiled to Assyria and Babylon according to the judgment laid out in His *Torah*, and it is during this time that the Bible tells us of the **Prophesied Kingdom**.[6] In the biblical writings of the prophets, a time is foretold when God would act decisively through His appointed King, the Messiah, who would fulfill all of His kingdom promises. However, while the Jews who returned from captivity under Ezra, Zerubbabel, and Nehemiah thought this would come to pass immediately, this **Prophesied Kingdom** was pointing towards the New Testament era.

The New Testament records the life and ministry of Jesus Christ, a descendant of king David and Abraham, and the ministry of his church. Jesus ministered four hundred years after the Old Testament had been completed, and in his teaching, he made clear by various forms that he was the long-awaited Messiah. The Old Testament teaches that the Messiah would come

4. Ibid.
5. Ibid., 24-25.
6. Ibid., 25.

as one who was divine and yet in the form of man, and the New Testament affirms this in presenting Jesus as the Son of God having come in human flesh. The study of Christology is vast in and of itself, but to read a few passages from the Old and New Testaments, we can discern the various forms of fulfillment:

In Daniel 7:13-14, for example, the prophet writes of the Messianic vision he received in 603 BCE:

> ...behold, with the clouds of heaven there came one like a son of man, and he came to the Ancient of Days and was presented before him. And to him was given dominion and glory and a kingdom, that all peoples, nations, and languages should serve him; his dominion is an everlasting dominion, which shall not pass away, and his kingdom one that shall not be destroyed.

When Jesus stood before the high priest in the first century AD, he was questioned as to who he truly was. Matthew records the interrogation:

> ...the high priest said to Him, "I charge You under oath by the living God: Tell us if You are the Christ, the Son of God." "You have said it yourself," Jesus answered. "But I say to all of you, from now on you will see the Son of Man sitting at the right hand of the Mighty One and coming on the clouds of heaven" (Matt. 26:63-64).

The prophet Isaiah, too, wrote of the coming Messiah in the mid 8th century BCE, prophesying:

> The Spirit of the Lord GOD is upon me, because the Lord has anointed me to bring good news to the poor; he has sent me to bind up the brokenhearted, to pro-

claim liberty to the captives, and the opening of the prison to those who are bound (Isa. 61:1).

The gospel writer Luke, in the first century AD, records that Jesus affirmed the personal fulfillment of this passage, having read it in the synagogue and stating to the congregants: "Today this Scripture has been fulfilled in your hearing" (Lk. 4:21).

In both of these circumstances (Matt. 26:63-64; Lk. 4:21), many of those in the crowd sought to kill Jesus, for he claimed equality with God. In fact, by the order of the high priest he was condemned to death. This undeniable claim to divinity by Jesus is further supported by John 8:57-58. In this passage the Jews asked:

> "You are not yet fifty years old, and You have seen Abraham?" "Truly, truly, I tell you," Jesus declared, "before Abraham was born, I am!"

These are but a few out of several passages which can be compared between the Old and New Testaments as to their fulfillment in Christ, but my preferred, perhaps for its revelatory detail and its redemptive significance, is the entire chapter of Isaiah 53 which prophesies of the Christ's suffering at the cross. He is the King who came as the prophesied Suffering Servant.

The crucifixion of the Christ was the fulfillment of God's promise in Genesis 3:15, for by fulfilling the law and being therefore sinless before God, Jesus was made a worthy sacrifice to pay the sin-debt of mankind. The breaking of God's law, after all, required a penalty because of God's absolute just nature, and by pouring out His wrath upon His Son, He could lawfully forgive man, satisfy justice, and by the resurrection power that raised Jesus from the dead, restore and sanctify man. God took on human flesh in order to fulfill that which God's people could not, so that redeemed man might, by the love, grace and mercy of God, enjoy the blessings of His righteous reign.

Jesus Christ, the anointed Messiah, the incarnate Son of God, had come to establish God's kingdom, the **Present Kingdom** which is both visible and hidden today.[7] It is visible in that Christians – consisting of all ethnicities, including believing Jews – reflect that they are God's people in their cultivation of God's creation and culture in honour of Christ their Lord, living lives that exhibit willful obedience to His law-word (the Bible). The kingdom is hidden, however, in that it is not yet fully made manifest, but upon Christ's return at the reserved time for the judgment, it will be made fully manifest in all of creation, the **Perfected Kingdom**.[8] This is the kingdom that is proclaimed by God's people, for it is by means of the kingdom of God that all creation will be redeemed and restored, beginning with the human heart.

In affirmation of the harmony and unity of Scripture in relation to its unfolding narrative, Norman L. Geisler, a Christian theologian, writes:

The 'Paradise Lost' of Genesis becomes the 'Paradise

---

7. Willem J. Ouweneel, *Power in Service: An Introduction to Christian Political Thought* (Jordan Station, ON.: Paideia Press, 2014), 4.

8. Roberts, *God's Big Picture*, 25.

Regained' of Revelation. Whereas the gate to the tree of life is closed in Genesis, it is opened forevermore in Revelation.[9]

The Bible, though written with human hands, is God's special revelation to man. By His Spirit, He inspired its authors to write the inerrant and infallible text. It is God's authoritative interpretation of reality, His living word, which penetrates the heart of man as a double-edged sword, confronting him with the truth about himself and his surroundings, and cutting down all falsehood. As such, being the word of God, it is without error, and cannot be false in what it teaches. This is what it claims about itself, and the true church has upheld this doctrine since its very conception.

1.3 The Cultural Contribution of the Bible

As a result, therefore, of what the Bible claims to be, Christians – who were historically the majority in the West – heavily relied on it as their foundation for the development of Western civilization. It was, in fact, what facilitated and motivated progress in the societal spheres. At root, this reliance upon God's word for public affairs can be traced back to the Roman Empire's adoption of the Christian faith as the state religion, but this was *not* its beginning. Historically, it began with the Garden of Eden, as Adam and Eve were tasked with cultivating creation into a godly civilization; and it continued with the nation of Israel in the Old Testament,

---

9.   Norman L. Geisler and William E. Nix, *A General Introduction to the Bible*, Revised and Expanded (Chicago, IL.: Moody Publishers, 2008), 28.

who relied upon God's word for the structure and direction of their civilization. But it was not until the protestant reformation (500 years ago) that the word of God was more faithfully applied over a much larger society in the West. This was not something *new*, but rather a *recovery* of a biblical mandate resulting from recovered biblical truths and principles that had been progressively revealed and applied in human history.

The Bible itself speaks of its comprehensive scope, where, for example, Zechariah 5:1-4 depicts a flying scroll of the law covering up an entire city. And in the apostle Paul's first letter to the Corinthians, he writes of the universal kingship of Christ and that he "must reign until he has put all his enemies under his feet. The last enemy to be destroyed is death. For 'God has put all things in subjection under his feet...'" (1 Cor. 15:25-27). It is in Zechariah's flying scroll that covers all, and Paul's words of the subjection of all things under Christ's feet, that we learn that God's word is authoritative and governing for man in *all* societal spheres, this is inclusive of family life, church, state, school, business, the arts, sciences, law, economics, politics and all else. *All* of reality is God's created reality, and therefore *all* things are subject to God's word revelation.

The Protestant reformer, Pierre Viret, wrote in his book *Christian Introduction in the Doctrine of the Law and the Gospel* that:

> God has included in this Law [Scripture] every aspect of that moral doctrine by which men may live well. For in these Laws he has done infinitely better than the Phi-

losophers and all their books, whether they deal with Ethics, Economics or Politics. This Law stands far above all human legislation, whether past, present or future and is above all laws and statutes edicted by men… This Law, if it is rightly understood, will furnish us with true Ethics, Economics and Politics.[10]

Viret's study of God's word uncovered the (i) comprehensive scope of the Christian faith; (ii) the all-encompassing Lordship of Christ; and (iii) the enduring relevance of His word revelation for man and every sphere of life. He did not advocate a *Biblicism*, which would have been an abuse of Scripture, but rather the wise and careful interpretation and application of biblical principles for the cultivation and later realization of a *true* culture, in which there might be *true* ethics, economics, politics, etc.

A *true* culture can only exist when it is structurally rooted in God's word and when the prevailing worship of the people is directionally oriented towards the true Creator God of the Bible. When culture deviates from its true direction and undermines its underlying foundation, culture cannot progress but instead *regress*, eventually to the point of disorganization and self-destruction.

From the moment that the Bible was disregarded as the answer to our culture's questions, and its claim of divine inspiration called into doubt, the West has, ever since, been undermining the sure foundation on

---

10. Pierre Viret, *Instruction chrétienne en la doctrine de la Loi et de l'Evangile* (Genève, 1564), 255.

which our society was built. We can consider, for example, the rule of law and the protection of the rights and dignity of the human person, which Indian philosopher, Vishal Mangalwadi, writes in his publication *The Book that Made your World* that:

> the covenant of the Ten Commandments founded the modern principle of constitutionalism, or rule of law, by a perpetual written and binding law. Britain's submission to the rule of law was institutionalized with the Magna Carta (1215), founded on common law, tracing to the code of Alfred the Great. The Mosaic code was the foundation for such legal codes in the West.[11]

The notion of "human dignity" was originally a Christian concept when we consider that it was Scripture that provided the underlying bedrock for the Declaration of Independence (which affirms the "inalienable right to life, liberty and the pursuit of happiness");[12] the UN Declaration of Human Rights (which recognizes the dignity and equality of man for "freedom, justice and peace");[13] the 2005 Constitution for Europe (which also affirms the inviolable rights of

---

11. Vishal Mangalwadi, *The Book that Made your World: How the Bible Created the Soul of Western Civilization* (Nashville: Thomas Nelson, 2011), 339.

12. National Archives and Records Administration, "Declaration of independence - Text Transcript," *The Charters of Freedom*. Accessed April 19, 2016, http://www.archives.gov/exhibits/charters/declaration_transcript.html.

13. United Nations, "The Universal Declaration of Human Rights," *United Nations*. Accessed April 19, 2016, http://www.un.org/en/universal-declaration-human-rights/.

human dignity);[14] and the Canadian Charter of Human Rights (which declare the "principles that recognize the supremacy of God and the rule of law").[15] Although these legal charters are not distinctly "Christian", in that they are structurally and religiously humanistic, without Scripture serving as the foundation for Western law, such charters would have never been developed and adopted. All that the liberal progressivists of the last few generations have done is inherit that which was produced by a Christian social order and attempt to redefine and reinterpret laws and rights contrary to the mandated norms of Scripture. They have, in other words, borrowed from the Christian worldview in order to build their secular and pagan versions of society. But instead of human progress, what we are witnessing is a regress into religious apostasy and moral rebellion, leading towards a disorganized social order.

It was the Anglican bishop Michael Nazir-Ali who wrote that:

> Even agnostic philosophers have said that, in the end, notions of inherent human dignity depend on the Judeao-Christian view that men and women have been created in God's image and that this can never be taken

---

14. European Communities, "Treaty Establishing a Constitution for Europe, 2005", *EU*. Accessed April 18, 2016 http://europa.eu/eu-law/decision-making/treaties/pdf/treaty_establishing_a_constitution_for_europe/treaty_establishing_a_constitution_for_europe_en.pdf.

15. Legislative Services Branch, "CONSTITUTION ACT, 1982," *Justice Laws Website*. Accessed April 19, 2016, http://laws-lois.justice.gc.ca/eng/Const/page-15.html.

away from them.[16]

When we think of the values of caring for the weak, the poor, the destitute, and those who are deemed by society as undeserving, this was and has always been at root a biblical principle which led to the establishment of hospitals, hospices, food and clothing banks. For when the plagues ravaged Europe, it was the Christians who stayed behind to tend to the sick even at the cost of their own lives. These are the biblical values which have been institutionalized in our culture and became a principle that was emulated by other cultures around the globe.[17] It is a principle which can only be sustained from within the Christian worldview, for by no other philosophy of life can such a principle emerge.

1.4 The Falling Away from Scriptural Authority (Pretended Autonomy)

The falling away from Scriptural authority in the West, however, was due in large part to the preceding synthesis (or combination) of biblical principles with foreign, antithetical thought systems. The Romanticism of the 18th century, for example, advocated a radical individualism which absolutized the emotional aspect of man, contrasting the rationalism of the Enlightenment. The subjective implications of Romanticism has, in many ways, shaped modernity in its existentialist thought,

---

16. Michael Nazir-Ali, *The Unique and Universal Christ: Jesus in a Plural World* (Colorado Springs, CO.: Paternoster, 2008), 3.

17. See Carlisle Percival, "The Imago Dei in Modern Healthcare", in *Jubilee: Recovering Biblical Foundations for Our Time*, ed. Joseph Boot, Spring 2012 (Toronto: Ezra Institute for Contemporary Christianity).

where René Descartes' "I think, therefore I am" has been replaced with "I *feel*, therefore I am." This thought is plainly evident in the present debates on gender, sexuality and the family, where one's "feelings" are absolutized as the subjective norm and objective standard for reality. But the modern social order has not only been influenced by Romanticism, but by the Enlightenment of the late 17th and early 18th century as well.

The philosophical movement of the Enlightenment primarily concerned itself with the absolutization of the intellectual aspect of man, and this implied two things: (i) discarding the Bible as the authoritative source for all knowledge; and (ii) proposing "reason" as man's "great saviour." The reason for discarding biblical authority was expressed in rationalist thought as man being able to arrive at true knowledge concerning reality, ethics and epistemology independently from religion (most particularly, Christianity).

The implications of Enlightenment thought were the fostering of an acceptance of secularism and religious neutrality in our present world, but there are *two fundamental problems* with rationalist thought. *Firstly,* by discarding God's authoritative revelation of reality, man is unable to make sense of the intelligibility of human experience. If we are God's creation, and we live in God's world, and we were created to live in and to govern this world, how can we possibly arrive at any true knowledge without presupposing the God who created us? This is not to say that we cannot arrive at *any* knowledge, but that we cannot *truly* know anything as long as we cannot make sense of anything.

The atheist, for example, who believes that the universe came about by causality, is required to explain how order can emerge from chaos; how laws (which are fixed and absolute) can exist in a universe governed by chance; and how moral values are meaningful in a universe that has no purpose or meaning. How does the godless secularist justify the uniformity of reality which we all presuppose?

Secondly, the "reason" of the Enlightenment is nothing more than an abstract concept which does not actually exist. This is not to be confused with man's intellectual capability "to understand." We can *understand* the text we read in a book; we can *understand* the data in a scientific journal; we can *understand* the news channel on television. We are *rational* creatures, do not mistake me as claiming that we are not. But the concept of "reason" is something beyond the intellect of man. We must ask: How do we know what "reason" is? How can we *agree* on what "reason" is? If two persons disagree on its definition, who is right? How do we know that the other is wrong? By what standard do we know this?

The abstract concept of "reason" was introduced in the West in order to replace the Bible as the ultimate authority for all knowledge. It is, at root, what Adam and Eve sought in the Garden of Eden, to determine for themselves what is moral (ethics), what is real (metaphysics), and what is true (knowledge), over against what God established for ethics, metaphysics and knowledge. The philosopher P. Andrew Sandlin explains how it was "reason" that led to the West's falling away from Scripture, in his book *Christian Culture*:

> ...the chief tenet of Enlightenment – that no author-
> ity could sit in judgment on human reason, that man's
> reason and experience were the measure of all things –
> suffocated Christian culture.[18]

As a result of the wayward direction of our culture, the Bible has gone from (point A) being the answer to our culture's questions, to (point B) being the
question of our culture. I might put it this way: It is
no longer God who judges, orders and guides man
through His law-word, but man who judges the word
of God. This is the prevailing perspective of our age:
structurally and directionally opposing the God of the
Bible, and upholding man as the measure of all things.
This is the *humanism* that defines our age, both religious
and secular.

Now, here is the point of conflict, or antithesis, between Christians and unbelievers: The former believes
and affirms that the Bible is the inspired and inerrant
word of God for all of life. The latter, however, believe
that the Bible is NOT the word of God but instead a
book that is solely the literary work of man. The former believes that we cannot know anything if not by
the revelation of God, and the latter believes that we
can know almost anything by "reason" and without the
help of the Bible. What could I possibly say to you
about this antithesis (or conflict)?

18. P. Andrew Sandlin, *Christian Culture: An Introduction* (Mount
Hermon, CA.: Center for Cultural Leadership, 2013), 23.

1.5 The Self-Witness of the Bible

Well, if you recall, I had said from the very beginning that my position is unashamedly that of the Christian reformers, principally, that I believe that the Bible is the inspired word of God, and that it is the fount of all wisdom and understanding. Let me explain to you why I believe that to be true:

In 2 Timothy 3:16, the apostle Paul states:

All Scripture is breathed out by God and profitable for teaching, for reproof, for correction, and for training in righteousness.

And in 2 Peter 1:20-21, the apostle Peter states:

...knowing this first of all, that no prophecy of Scripture comes from someone's own interpretation. For no prophecy was ever produced by the will of man, but men spoke from God as they were carried along by the Holy Spirit.

There are several other passages which affirm this same message, which to summarize is that, based on the inspiration of the text, "the Bible itself claims to be the Word of God." We can also refer to this as the self-attestation of the Bible, in which *the Christian Scriptures bears witness of its own inspiration.*

Now, of course, I am well aware of what objections generally come to mind when such a statement is made:

1. The Bible's own claim to be the word of God cannot be considered valid;

2. The evidence must first be weighed to prove the truthfulness of this statement;

3. This is circular reasoning, and therefore invalid.

1.5.1 The Self-Attestation of Scripture

To begin with, a holy book is not "inspired" (breathed out by God) because someone says it is. For example, the Vedas of the Hindus, or the Pali Canon of the Buddhists, do not claim to be the inspired or dictated word of god (which in their case are the impersonal gods Brahman and Nirvana). If all the Hindus or Buddhists were to claim that these were the words of god, this would not make them the words of God. If the majority of humanity were to claim that these were the words of god, this would not make them so. The truthfulness of a statement is not determined by what the majority believes. And if the books themselves do not claim to be the breathed-out words of god, then they can never be considered the words of god. And who is man to say that they are the words of god?

The Bible, however, does claim to be the word of God. And because it makes this claim, as rational creatures in God's created world, we are able to verify if this claim is true by asking the following questions:

1. Is it internally consistent?

2. Does it adequately explain the condition of man and our fallen world?

3. By adopting its presuppositions (that is to say, by presupposing its truth), does it explain the intelligibility of human experience?

We must first begin with what the Bible claims about itself, and then study its correspondence to reality to verify its claim. As long as we begin with the same presuppositions as Scripture (presupposing its truth), we will find that 100% of the time it will show itself to be true. If we were to do this with any other religious book, however, we will find that 100% of the time it will show itself to be false. I intend to delve into this in the next lecture, "Jesus amongst other gods", for now, bear with me with this bold assertion.

1.5.2 Evidences & Facts: The Myth of Neutrality

At this point, you may be saying to yourself, "But that is only because you are presupposing its truth, what about being neutral in your thinking and then consulting the extra-biblical evidence? Follow the evidence wherever it leads!" This is the second objection I had mentioned, and let me explain to you, in two points, the fault in this approach.

At first, this might sound noble and fair, but to be "neutral" is solely theoretical and an impossibility to realize. You cannot be neutral when consulting evidences and facts, because whenever you interact with an evidence or fact, you are interpreting it from your own worldview. You already have beliefs regarding ethics, metaphysics, and epistemology. You are not a "blank slate," the Enlightenment's *tabula rasa*. You are just as religious as the person beside you, with your own presuppositions. To put your beliefs and presuppositions aside is like the bird removing its wings or the leopard losing its spots. You and your presuppositions are inseparable, the only way to eliminate the one is to eliminate the other – and that doesn't sound very appealing, does it?

The truth of the matter is that, all humanity, irrespective of what they claim to believe (or whether they have even been exposed to the Christian faith), presuppose the God of the Bible in their living and thinking. We all presuppose the uniformity of human experience (i.e., I expect food to digest when I eat it; or I expect water to boil when I heat it; or I expect toothpaste to eject when I squeeze the container). There is a uniformity to reality, a sequence of events we come to expect, the cause and effect relationship, and all other factors that are therein involved. This reflects God's creational law, which in turn reflects God's existence, and His logically consistent character.

We also presuppose the laws of logic, such as the law of non-contradiction. For example, when I say that (1) the Male is not a Female; and (2) the Female is a Male; only one of these statements can be true in the same sense. They cannot both be true in the same sense. If we deny the law of non-contradiction, then intelligible discourse would be impossible. We also have the law of identity, which is not to be ignored, for if I refer to a "cat", I do not mean a "dog." Language would break down if it were purely subjective. This too reflects God's creational law, which in turn reflects God's existence, and His logically consistent character.

We effectually presuppose the biblical God in our thinking and living, because only by presupposing God can we (i) live and think in God's created world, and

(ii) make sense of the intelligibility of human experience. I will, again, elaborate on this in the next lecture, but for now, to summarize my argument in just a few short words that would otherwise not distract me from the subject of this lecture, it was Greg L. Bahnsen, the apologist of the 20th century, who echoed the philosophy of his teacher, Cornelius Van Til, that *the proof of the Christian worldview is the impossibility of the contrary.*

Consider this reality: We all presuppose the biblical God in our thinking and living because we know Him to be true, and we have this knowledge by virtue of (i) being created in His image (that is to say, we are like Him as much as a creature can be), and (ii) by the natural revelation of the world around us. His word revelation is one of the two aspects of God's unified revelation (the other being "created reality"). And these two revelations presuppose and supplement one another.

But *why* is the Bible the *authoritative* interpretation of created reality? Is not God's natural revelation sufficient? In one sense, it is sufficient as it makes clear to us that our world is not what it ought to be, and all of creation bears the fingerprints of the Creator. In another sense, it is not sufficient because it does not communicate how man might be redeemed from his fallen and broken condition (hence God's written revelation). Natural revelation was always meant to be one of the two aspects of God's unified revelation, so we would be wrong to separate it from God's special, written revelation.

The necessity of Scripture is also explained in the writings of Paul in Romans 1, who explains that, though we know the truth of God, we suppress this truth by our hostility towards God. We presuppose Him in our thinking and living, but we deny Him in our professed worldviews (or presuppositions). We are walking, talking contradictions.

This suppression of the truth is partly why the Bible was given to man, because without it, the *noetic effects* of sin (that is to say, the corrupting influence of sin on the human mind) would make it impossible for man alone to interpret correctly God's natural revelation in creation. We would always seek to replace the true Creator God for some aspect of His creation, and for this reason, an authoritative interpretation of God's created reality was required from the Creator Himself.

To summarize my first point on this: Neutral thinking is an impossibility. We are either subject in obedience to God, or set up in hostility towards Him. As a result, whatever evidence or facts we may come across will either be interpreted in agreement with God's unified revelation, or misinterpreted (and even twisted) to deny or run contrary to God's unified revelation. This brings us to the second point.

1.5.3 Evidences & Facts: No Brute Facts

As it concerns extra-biblical evidences and facts, which are normally requested by skeptics and unbelievers for the claim of the truthfulness and trustworthiness of Scripture, we must first address the philosophy *underlying* evidences and facts. Let me explain why.

I could present before you the fact that there are more ancient manuscript copies for the Old and New

Testament than any other work of antiquity.[19] In fact, there are over 28,000 New Testament manuscripts in various ancient languages, such as Coptic, Greek, Latin, Syriac and more – whereas Homer's *Iliad* only has 643 manuscript copies. The science of textual criticism has even confirmed that 99% of manuscripts are accurate, with the 1% only being slips of the pen or minor grammatical mistakes. Dr. Bart Ehrman, a scholar who denies the inspiration of the Bible, even wrote:

> Most of the changes found in our early Christian manuscripts have nothing to do with theology or ideology.[20]

Perhaps in response to the evidence presented before you, and after having done some research yourself, you might agree that the Bible is the most well-preserved work of antiquity with an overwhelming amount of archaeological support. But that will not have convinced you that the Bible is the *word* of God. It does not challenge your *worldview*, what you believe about reality, ethics and truth.

I could also present substantial evidence for the resurrection of Jesus, dispelling the theories of a fake death, of hallucinations, and that of a hidden identical twin. I can make a solid case that the gospels are the testimonies of eyewitnesses, as excellently laid out

19. See Joseph M. Holden, *The Popular Handbook of Archaeology and the Bible: Discoveries that Confirm the Reliability of Scripture* (Eugene, OR.: Harvest House Publishers, 2013).
20. Bart Ehrman, *Misquoting Jesus: The Story Behind Who Changed the Bible and Why* (New York, NY.: Harper San Francisco, 2005), 55.

by scholar Richard Bauckham,[21] and that every event (even the supernatural) took place in history – and you may even accept all this. But this does not mean that you accept the Bible as the word of God, does it? You might say, "Yes it seems irrefutable that Jesus arose from the dead, and that he performed many miracles, but so what? Weird things happen in our world, we are just not able to explain them yet."

You might even reject all these evidences and facts because you require more evidences for the evidences I present before you. If I present a piece of evidence called "A", you'll want evidence to verify "A", so I present you with the evidence "B" to verify "A". But now you want evidence to verify "B", so I present you with the evidence "C" to verify "B". This could go on for an infinity. But this is not how we reason, is it? If I tell you that it is sunny outside, you might look for yourself and verify that it is true. You are not going to ask for evidence that your eyes are working properly, and that your mind is receiving the right image, and that the image is in fact a sunny sky. At some point, we all refer to some ultimate authority for our certainty.

Two points need to be made here: (1) Evidences and facts are not neutral, abstract, and impersonal. If they were, then evidences would be nothing more than undifferentiated data, and we would not be able to explain why such evidences are intelligible to the human mind. In fact, they would be unintelligible by impli-

---

21. See Richard Bauckham, *Jesus and the Eyewitnesses: The Gospels as Eyewitness Testimony*, second ed. (Grand Rapids, MI.: W.B. Eerdmans, 2017).

cation. Instead, evidences and facts are personal, objective, created facts because we live in God's world. They are (in other words) *God's facts*. This means that they have an objective meaning because they are part of God's natural revelation, and so we either interpret evidences and facts truthfully as they are (as guided by God's word), or we borrow them and misinterpret them altogether in order to support a false philosophy of life.

1.5.4 Circular Reasoning

As it concerns circular reasoning, well, the truth of the matter is, (2) we cannot avoid circular reasoning as it concerns our ultimate authority for certainty. For many, man's "reason" is his ultimate authority. He is the measure of all things. And so, as opposed to the Christian's answer "Because the Bible says so," the rationalist will say "Because that is the conclusion of reason" or "Because I have reasoned so." Arguing that the Bible's self-witness to its divine inspiration is circular reasoning is not a valid objection when every argument about our ultimate epistemological authority is circular in itself.

We see this, for example, when asking: Does our professed worldview, or that of Scripture, prove its own conclusions using its own standards? Those who believe that human reason is the ultimate authority must presuppose the authority of reason in their arguments for rationalism. Those who believe in the ultimate authority of our sense experience must presuppose that same authority in arguing for empiricism.

And for those who are skeptics, they must be skeptical about their skepticism in order to be consistent. As the reformed philosopher John M. Frame writes:

> The point is that when one is arguing for an ultimate criterion, whether Scripture, the Qur'an, human reason, sensation, or whatever, one must use criteria compatible with that conclusion. If that is circularity, then everybody is guilty of circularity.[22]

If we were to conduct an honest study of the world religions, what we would discover is that, every worldview, every philosophy of life, apart from Scripture, hijacks itself and fails to prove its own conclusions about what is real, what is moral and what is true by its own standards and presuppositions. And that is because they cannot stand on their own, they must borrow capital from the Christian, biblical worldview in order to somehow function. Consider this fact as we work through three prominent religious worldviews in our next lecture together.

1.6 The Tonic of the Bible

It is in light of a fallen and broken world, with a culture that is regressing towards structural instability, that I stand here, as the church has historically done, to call every listener to the truth of God's word in hope for the restoration of God's creation. The Bible, as the inspired word of God, rightly interprets our world as in need of redemption and restoration. And being with-

---

22. John M. Frame, "Why Everyone is Guilty of the Circular Argument." *P&R Books*. Accessed April 19, 2016, https://www.prpbooks.com/blog/2015/08/10376/.

out error, being true in all it teaches, the word revelation of God is the absolute authority for all knowledge, guiding man in his study and cultivation of all the aspects of God's creation, and instructing him in the way of salvation in Jesus Christ – a restoration which is not only for the person, but for the whole created order.

If we hope to have a true understanding of reality, of morality and of knowledge; and recover the biblical principles upon which Western civilization was built in order that we might reform human culture, then we must return to the principle of *Sola Scriptura*, restoring the position of Scripture to its rightful place as the ultimate authority for all life and thought – and not just in the church, but in every aspect and sphere of society. It is only then that we might truly cultivate a *true* culture, rightly oriented towards the Creator God of Scripture. For only by loving God can we effectively love fellow man.

This return to *Sola Scriptura*, however, first involves a renunciation of our pretended autonomy, this false belief that we can somehow be neutral, independent from God, and judge what is real, moral and true (as established by God). It involves a complete surrender to the absolute authority of God's word, repenting of our sin (our violations of God's law), and placing our faith in what Christ has done on the cross for the sinner's salvation. When we submit to his Kingship and are renewed by the grace and power of God, we will then be able to apply this grace and transformative power to every work we put our hands to do. For this has been man's calling since the beginning, as the

Bible tells us, to cultivate God's creation into a godly civilization, extending His kingdom to the ends of the earth. As theologians term this, the "cultural mandate", which was renewed in the Great Commission (Matt. 28:18-20).

This is the gospel (the good news) of Scripture, the restoration of man in God's image for the recovery of his calling and purpose; to preserve and advance the goodness, truth and beauty of God's kingdom, reclaiming creation as the theatre of God's glory.

Without the authoritative revelation of God which interprets, presupposes and supplements God's natural revelation in creation, man will forever be lost in his false philosophies and illusions – chasing after the wind. He will know not his true purpose, will fail to find the meaningfulness in his everyday work, and will drown in his own futility and misery – desperately trying to comprehend reality, morality and knowledge independently from God, but always failing because he cannot help but presuppose God in his living and thinking. And if, in the end, he resolves himself to reject God's sovereign revelation, to reject Christ, who is the focal point of its unfolding redemptive history, to reject the Saviour of the world and Lord of all creation, he will thus be judged and found guilty for having defied the law of the universal King, for being a gross and vile sinner. For true justice demands judgment.

In parting, my dear listeners, I plead that you heed my words: It is only by obeying and applying the comprehensive scope of the inspired word of God that the structure and direction of human life and thought might be rightly oriented and realized. There is no other fount of life, wisdom and understanding for men to turn to as their ultimate authority. May the Bible be your life's foundation.

LECTURE 2

Jesus Amongst
Other Gods

*"Yet for us there is one God, the Father, from whom are all
things and for whom we exist, and one Lord, Jesus Christ,
through whom are all things and through whom we exist."*

– 1 Corinthians 8:6

2.1 Introduction

I CANNOT RECOUNT HOW MANY times it has been now
that I have been asked to speak on "Jesus amongst
other gods." Whether it is back in North America, in
the Caribbean, or somewhere in Ibero-America, it has
continued to be a popular subject. I imagine that it has
a lot to do with the predominance of religious pluralism in the West, and all the sorts of questions that it
raises – such as:

- How do we understand the claims of Jesus
  compared to the claims of other religious figures?

- How should we regard the relationship of
  Christianity with culture given the presence of
  other religions in society?

- And, should a synthesis be considered for the preservation of the human religion?

These have been questions that I have continually fielded, and no other subject has, perhaps, garnered as much controversy as the exclusivity of the Christian faith.

What times we are living in. It is literally a night and day comparison when we look back at the period of Christendom. The societal structure and direction of the West was, a few centuries ago, predominantly Christian. But when the Western world turned its attention to the influences of Romanticism and the Enlightenment – the former concerning itself with the absolutization of human "feeling" and the individual, and the latter with the absolutization of man's "reason" – the Christian God was regarded by the spirit of change as an enemy of true progress and realization. Man was to be the *measure* of all things, but the God of Christian theism stood in his way. The French atheist, Voltaire (1694-1778), for example, believed that the first step towards human progress involved entirely casting off biblical authority and the Christian religion.[1]

But the rationalism and secularization of human life that followed the eighteenth-century left mankind – not without a religion, for he had merely adopted the religion of humanism – but without a spirituality. And for this reason, before World War I, there was a hunger for, and a renewed interest in a sort of "spirituality"

1. See Voltaire, *Oeuvres Complètes de Voltaire, Volume 7*, ed. Georges Avenel (Paris: Aux Bureaux du Siècle, 1869).

for the West, eventually culminating in the World's first Parliament of Religions of 1893. This gathering was first proposed to be man's quest for the truth, where the Ba'hai, the Hindu, the Sikh, the Christian, and the Muslim would arrive at some agreement about a common *spirituality* after lengthy discussion, but this was merely the dawn of the West's religious pluralism – the beginning of the philosophy that "All religious roads lead to Rome".

Charles C. Bonney, spokesperson for the World's Parliament of Religions, opened the first historic assembly by stating:

> This day the sun of a new era of religious peace and progress rises over the world, dispelling the dark clouds of sectarian strife. This day a new flower blooms in the gardens of religious thought, filling the air with its exquisite perfume. This day a new fraternity is born into the world of human progress, to aid in the upbuilding of the kingdom of God in the hearts of men. Era and flower and fraternity bear one name. It is a name which will gladden the hearts of those who worship God and love man in every clime. Those who hear its music joyfully echo it back to sun and flower. It is the Brotherhood of Religions.[2]

The Great War, however, brought a momentary pause to the World's Parliament of Religions. While its

---

2. Charles Carroll Bonney, "Words of Welcome," in *The Dawn of Religious Pluralism: Voices from the World's Parliament of Religions, 1893*, ed. Richard Hughes Seager (La Salle, IL.: Open Court Publishing Company, 1993), 21-22.

participants sought peace by means of common religion, the world was cast into violent chaos. But for its first ever gathering, it had proved sufficient enough to culturally influence the direction of the West towards a state of mind where religions could be regarded as equals, and presently, where religions might equally contribute towards the development of society. As the philosophy scholar, Lenn E. Goodman, writes in his book *Religious Pluralism and Values in the Public Sphere*:

> [The] pluralist thesis says: There is room in a society for divergent values, practices, and beliefs, even in many central areas of human concern.[3]

Since the departure from a Christian social order, the West has gone from rejecting Christian truth toward synthesizing it with other diverse religious worldviews, adopting the pluralist thesis. The Christ of the Christians has been lumped in with Muhammad, Krishna, and Buddha, and the Bible with other religious books as well. However, the truthfulness of a statement, or of a religion, is not based on what the majority believes. Truth is never determined by the majority. If we seek to know the truth about Jesus Christ, and not what the pluralist West has depicted him to be, we must turn to his own words and to his own works. And we will find that both his being and his words set the parameters by which we might understand the world, furnishing us with a true philosophy of life, consisting of a right perception of reality, morality and knowledge.

---

3.   Lenn E. Goodman, *Religious Pluralism and Values in the Public Sphere* (New York.: Cambridge University Press, 2014), 2.

2.2 The Person of Jesus

The gospel writers of the first century, Matthew, Mark, Luke and John, recorded the teaching and events of the life of Jesus. In Matthew and John's case, they were direct eyewitnesses. In Mark and Luke's case, they interviewed other eyewitnesses. Altogether, the gospels form a unified historical account of Jesus which has been verified time and again by extra-biblical evidence.

Although the exact words of what were said in many of these events may not have been written, the same message was nonetheless faithfully recorded and is found to be in harmony across all four gospels. Where one writer, for example, prefers to use the term "Kingdom of God", the other uses the term "Kingdom of heaven". They nonetheless mean the same thing. And when a writer decides to focus primarily on the persecution of Jesus by the two thieves crucified on the cross, another writer decides to focus on the later repentance of one of the thieves. What we have in the gospels is a beautiful mosaic of different writing styles, highlighted events, and teachings, all communicating a single narrative of the life and ministry of Jesus.

A critical study of these gospels would provide us with all we need to learn about the true personhood of Jesus and who he claimed to be. In consideration of the time I have available, however, a summary would be most sufficient. In their book, *Putting Jesus in His Place,* New Testament scholars Robert Bowman Jr. and Ed Komoszewski outline that there are five main traits of Jesus' life that affirm his claim of being the Son of God.[4]

---

4.   Robert Bowman Jr. and Ed Komoszewski, *Putting Jesus In*

2.3 The Five Traits of Jesus

The **first** trait is Jesus sharing "the honours due to God." In Matthew's gospel, for example, Jesus quotes Deuteronomy 6:13 when he was tempted in the wilderness: "Worship the LORD your God, and serve only Him" (Matt. 4:10). But throughout that gospel, we read of Jesus being the object of worship (2:2, 11; 8:2; 9:18; 14:33; 15:25; 20:20; 28:9, 17).[5] When Jesus walked on water, calmed the sea, and saved Peter (his disciple) from drowning, Matthew writes "Then those who were in the boat came and worshiped Him, saying, 'Truly You are the Son of God'" (14:33). And when Jesus asked the disciples who they believed he was, Simon Peter confessed "You are the Christ, the Son of the living God" (16:16). And after the bodily resurrection of the Christ, the disciples gathered on a mount in Galilee and "when they saw Him, they worshiped Him" (28:17). These are but a few examples as to how Jesus shared the honours due to God.

The **second** trait is Jesus sharing "the attributes of God." Not only is Jesus worshiped equally as God, but he also bears the nature of God.[6] When Jesus spoke with his disciples in John 14:9-10a, he said:

> "Have I been with you so long, and yet you have not known Me, Philip? He who has seen Me has seen the Father; so how can you say, 'Show us the Father'? Do you not believe that I am in the Father, and the Father in Me?"

His Place: The Case for the Deity of Christ (Grand Rapids, MI: Kregel Publications, 2007), 23.

5. Ibid., 38.
6. Ibid., 78.

What Jesus was teaching his disciples was that he is the perfect revelation of the Father, and having therefore seen Jesus, the disciples had seen the Father, who is God.

In another conversation, Jesus instructed his disciples that he existed well before he was born in human flesh. As we read in John 16:28:

"I came forth from the Father and have come into the world. Again, I leave the world and go to the Father."

In identifying Jesus as the *Logos* (Greek for the 'Word'), John 1:1 states that Jesus has been since the beginning, just as Genesis 1:1 asserts, that the *Logos* was with God, and the *Logos* was God. As commentator Donald MacLeod writes, "the Son is the *Logos* and the *Logos* has no origin."[7]

We also see that, in being able to turn stones into bread (Matt. 4:3-4), and multiplying five loaves of bread to feed five thousand men and their families (John 6:1-14), Jesus exhibits the omnipotence of God. And in perceiving the deep thoughts of the Pharisees when he had healed a paralytic, Jesus also exhibits the omniscience of God. As Mark 2:8-9 reads:

When Jesus perceived in His spirit that they reasoned thus within themselves, He said to them, "Why do you reason about these things in your hearts? Which is easier, to say to the paralytic, 'Your sins are forgiven you,' or to say, 'Arise, take up your bed and walk'?"

---

7. Donald MacLeod, *The Person of Christ: Contours of Christian Theology* (Downers Grove, IL.: InterVarsity Press, 1998), 73.

The fact that he could forgive the paralytic his sins exhibited Jesus' authority as that of God's, for not only could he heal the man's paralysis, but forgive his sins as the lawgiver whose law had been violated. In all these examples, we see how Jesus shared the attributes of God.

The **third** trait is Jesus sharing the very "names of God." When the disciple Thomas had seen and touched the resurrected Christ, John 20:28 records that he exclaimed "My Lord and my God!" This was not an expression of amazement, but as grammarians and lexicographers have affirmed, this was a direct *worship* of Jesus.[8]

Jesus is also called 'Immanuel,' in fulfillment of the messianic prophecy in Isaiah 7:14, which means "God with us." Jesus is the Son of God *incarnate*, having entered time from eternity and maintaining his full deity while walking the earth as fully human.

We can even consider the ministry of John the Baptist "preparing the way for the Lord Jesus," which had been foretold in Isaiah 40:3:

> The voice of one crying in the wilderness: 'Prepare the way of the LORD; make straight in the desert a highway for our God.

Not in any of these circumstances did Jesus correct his followers and listeners, in fact, he went on to even claim to be the great "I AM" as recorded in John 8:24,

---

8. Murray J. Harris, *Jesus as God: The New Testament Use of Theos in Reference to Jesus* (Eugene, OR.: Wipf & Stock Publishers), 110.

28 and v. 58. These were direct references to Exodus 3:14, where God had told Moses that He is the "I AM who I AM." These are just some of several examples as to how Jesus shared the names of God.

The **fourth** trait is Jesus sharing the "deeds that God does". As we read in John 1:1, Jesus was in the beginning with God, and all things were made through him. This meant that Jesus was active in the creation of the cosmos, an activity only attributable to God. And in his acts of miracles and healing, raising the dead, calming the storms, and much more, what differentiated Jesus from his disciples and the Old Testament prophets was that, where his followers and those before him had to appeal to God for the miraculous, Jesus was the authority himself.[9]

And given that only God can provide salvation, in John 14:6, Jesus states "I AM the way, the truth and the life. No one comes to the Father except through Me." In the book of Acts, we read that the early Christian community referred to the Christian faith as part of "the Way" (9:2; 19:9, 23; 22:4; 24:14, 22; cf. Acts 16:17; 18:25-26), in which it was understood that Jesus is the only "Way" of salvation.[10] But for those who are familiar with the Old Testament text, God does not share His glory with anyone. In this we see how Jesus shares in the deeds that God does, and God wills it so. God is not jealous when His Son claims to be equal with Him-

---

9. R. France, *The Gospel of Mark: A Commentary on the Greek Text, NIGTC* (Grand Rapids, MI.: Wm.B. Eerdman's Publishing, 2002), 370.

10. Bowman Jr. and Komoszewski, *Putting Jesus In His Place*, 208.

self in both being and deed, instead, He is delighted.

And finally, the **fifth** trait is Jesus sharing in the "seat of God's throne". In Mark's gospel, when Jesus is placed on trial by the Jewish Sanhedrin, the High Priest Caiaphas asked Jesus "Are you the Christ, the Son of the Blessed?" (Mk. 14:61b). Jesus responded "I am. And you will see the Son of Man sitting at the right hand of the Power, and coming with the clouds of heaven," which prompted the High Priest to tear his clothes and accuse him of blasphemy (vv. 63-64).

Two points can be made here, first, the title "Son of Man" is in reference to the messianic prophecy of Daniel 7:13, of "one like a son of man, coming with the clouds of heaven." Secondly, scholar Darrel L. Bock states that "[T]he image of riding the clouds is reserved for God... outside of this text in Daniel (Ex. 14:20; 34:5; Num. 10:34; Ps. 104:3; Isa. 19:1)... the image shows how intimately the function of the Son of Man is tied to divine authority even though the description is of a human."[11] We also read in Hebrews 12:2 that Jesus "endured the cross, disregarding its shame, and has taken his seat at the right hand of the throne of God."

And so we find in God's revealed word that Jesus shares (i) the honours due to God, (ii) the attributes of God, (iii) the names of God, (iv) the deeds of God, and (iv) the seat of God's throne.

---

11. Darrell L. Bock, *Jesus According to Scripture: Restoring the Portrait from the Gospels* (Grand Rapids, MI.: Baker Publishing Group, 1990), 345-346.

2.4 The Threefold Claims of Christ

In light of these five traits, the most definitive statement of Christ, which summarizes who he is and what he means for the world, is found in John 14:6, where he says: "I am the way, the truth and the life." And this is no ordinary statement, because no other religious figure in all the world has ever claimed to be: (1) the exclusive way of salvation (and to God); (2) the standard bearer of truth; and (3) the source of all life. You may find one or two who claim one of these three things, but no one has ever made this threefold claim about themselves. The Christian faith revolves around the very person of Christ because he *is* who he claims to be, the Saviour, the Son of God, and the Lord over all creation.

However, in claiming to be the way of salvation, we must ask the question "Salvation from what?" And in claiming to be the truth, we must ask "What is the truth?" And in claiming to be the way, we must also ask "What makes Christ the only way to God?"

In order to answer these questions, we need a basic understanding of the biblical worldview, otherwise we are not able to understand the words of Christ as he meant them. Christ, after all, was also a rabbi (a teacher of the *Torah*), and he upheld the Old Testament as historical and divinely inspired, operating within the parameters of its own worldview. For those not familiar with the term, a *worldview* can be defined as:

A network of presuppositions (which are not verified by the procedures of natural science) regarding reality (metaphysics), knowing (epistemology), and conduct (ethics) in terms of which every element of human experience is related and interpreted.[12]

Everyone has a worldview, a set of presuppositions (or what we believe to be true), by which we interpret human experience. The biblical worldview is that which the Bible teaches to be true.

According to the Bible, mankind was created in the *imago Dei* (the image of God), and bearing God's image, man was given authority to govern the earth subject to God's just governance. The historical Adam and Eve are the first parents of mankind, and they knew from the very beginning that God was the Creator, and that they were part of the creation. There was a clear distinction between Creator and creation, and this distinction is maintained throughout Scripture (we might call this *Two-ism*). To say that man was created in the *imago Dei* meant that he resembled God as much as a creature possibly could, but he did not, in any way, share the same essence as the Creator.

Now, Adam and Eve were given a command, that although they could eat the fruit of any tree in God's creation, they were not to eat the fruit of a particular tree (the tree of knowledge), and this was not because the tree itself was mystical or special. It was a tree just like any other tree. Why was this tree just as natural as the rest? Because, by obeying God's command towards

---

12. Gary DeMar, ed., *Pushing the Antithesis: The Apologetic Methodology of Greg L. Bahnsen* (Powder Springs, GA.: American Vision Press, 2010), 42-43.

this forbidden tree, they would then know how to be obedient in their interactions with the other aspects of God's creation. The real act of disobedience was not, however, in the eating of its fruit, but in our first parents' decision to discard God's moral law so that they might determine for themselves what was right and wrong. The fall of Adam and Eve, therefore, is rooted in their pursuit for complete independence from God, and this meant existential, epistemological, and moral independence – to be like God in a way that was unbefitting for a creature.

This disobedience is what the Bible calls "sin", and this act of sin has ravaged the totality of man's being. As the theologian Geerhardus Vos puts it, sin has caused a "radical reversal" in man, because as he has fallen from that which he was originally disposed, he has been diverted from his true nature and destiny, leading him towards disorganization and spiritual death. In his own words, the "process of dissolution."[13] This means that, in the falling away from original righteousness, what takes its place as the "natural" state of man is unrighteousness, and this comes with its curse, which the earth itself has also been subjected to.

The fallen condition of man, however, is not the full judgment of God. No, it is only partial. There awaits a judgment for all those who have sinned against God, for having broken His *Torah* which was given to Moses, and which is revealed through His creation

---

13. Geerhardus Vos, *Reformed Dogmatics, Vol. Two: Anthropology*, ed. Richard B. Gaffin, Jr., trans. Richard B. Gaffin, Jr. et al. (Grand Rapids, MI.: Lexham Press, 2012), 14.

(what some theologians call "creational law"). The just nature of God requires that the penalty for breaking the law be paid, and the penalty is death (Gen. 2:17; Rom. 6:23). The coming of Christ, therefore, is not only to teach us of true righteousness and the will of God, but to redeem and justify man according to the law, that he might not suffer the wrath of God on the day of judgment. This is why Christ stepped in from eternity and took on human flesh, that he might succeed where we have failed, that he might fulfill the law when we could not, so that by the crucifixion, God's wrath reserved for sinners may be laid upon the perfect and blameless man. He is the only person in all of human history who has no blemish, who has not committed a sin, and who lived a perfectly holy life on earth. As the patristic Athanasius wrote:

> [Christ] took to Himself a body, a human body even as our own. Nor did He will merely to become embodied or merely to appear; had that been so, He could have revealed His divine majesty in some other and better way. No, He took our body… He, the Mighty One, the [Creator] of all, Himself prepared this body in the virgin as a temple for Himself, and took it for His very own, as the instrument through which He was known and in which He dwelt. Thus, taking a body like our own, because all our bodies were liable to the corruption of death, He surrendered His body to death in place of all, and offered it to the Father. This he did out of sheer love for us.[14]

---

14. Cited in *St. Athanasius on the Incarnation: The Treatise "De Incarnatione Verbi Dei*, trans. and ed. A Religious of CSMV

Christ, therefore, offers salvation to all those who repent of their sin and submit to his Lordship, that by his salvation man might not only gain right standing with God again, but that he might recover his true purpose, which is, as God's prophet, to rightly interpret created reality after God; as God's priest, to dedicate creation and that which is cultivated (that is to say, culture) unto God; and as God's king, to govern creation subject to God's law-word.

There remains, however, the question of truth. What did Christ mean by "truth"? When questioned by Pontius Pilate, Jesus said "For this purpose I was born and for this purpose I have come into the world – to bear witness to the truth. Everyone who is of the truth listens to my voice" (Jn. 18:37). Pilate answered with a question, "What is truth?" (v. 38). If his question were to have been genuine, he would have surely stayed for the answer. Alas, he did not.

Truth is that which *is*. And it is exclusive. To make an assertion is to deny its opposite. Christ came to affirm the truth of the Old Testament, that we are all, in fact, God's creation, created in the *imago Dei*. He also affirmed our fallen condition, and the inevitable hostility that we have towards God as a result of our fallenness. But he did not come to solely testify to the truth of things outside of himself, he came as the very embodiment of truth. Just as he had come as God the Saviour, so he had also come as God the Creator, for all things in created reality can only be rightly interpreted

(Crestwood, N.Y.: St. Vladimir's Seminary Press, 1953 [orig. 1944]), 33-34.

when His word is referred to as the ultimate authority. In other words, God has established the truth, and his truth is revealed through His word (special revelation) and through creation (natural revelation) as one unified revelation. The nature of truth itself is determined by the logically consistent character of God, our Creator.

The word of the Creator, therefore, is true. For not only did God create all things, but according to the apostle Paul, "He is before all things, and in him all things hold together" (Col. 1:17). The right, true perception of reality, of knowledge and of ethics is that which God has established, and we can attain such a perception if we heed to God's word as the ultimate authority for all knowledge. All other philosophies of life (for this is what constitutes a philosophy of life) are *false* perceptions of reality, knowledge and ethics. Even if we attempt to arrive at the truth independently from God, we cannot help but suppress the truth as a result of our sinful nature (Rom. 1:18). This is why the word of God is the *only* authoritative interpretation of reality, for only by aligning our presuppositions to the truth of God's word can we rightly perceive the world as it truly is.

Finally, we arrive at the final question, "What makes Christ the only way to God?" Aside from being God himself, as part of the Triune godhead, he is also the only one capable of building a bridge between man and God, a bridge that spans the great chasm between them.

Let me explain: In the Garden of Eden, when our first parents sinned, they had, as a result, severed their relational connection with God. This meant that, on his own, man could never reason his way back to the biblical God. His sinful rebellion prevented him from doing so. This is why he may often arrive at some intended theism in his reasoning, but never the *Christian* theism. By doing this, that is, intentionally arriving at any deity, or none at all, as opposed to the true God of Scripture, man could essentially maintain his pretended autonomy, and preserve his pretended "godship" as being the determiner of what is real, moral and known.

When he does, however, arrive at Christian theism, this is not of his own doing, but rather the work of God who rescues him from his helpless and blind condition. And having been renewed from within, with his eyes having been opened to the truth, man is then able to renounce his pretended autonomy and embrace God as the Lord over all creation (including over his own thinking). But the means by which this is possible is in the person of Christ, who not only builds a bridge intellectually between man and God (as providing the authoritative interpretation of reality), but relationally as well. How so?

Given the holy and just nature of God, sinful man cannot share his presence with the Holy of Holies because it would kill him, and I mean that quite literally. Consider, for example, why Moses was hid behind a rock in order to see the glory of God pass before him, and even then he was not permitted to see God face to face (Exod. 33:12-23). In order to better understand this, we might use the analogy of the sun: We can see the daylight when we walk on the face of the earth, but we cannot look at the sun directly, it would blind us. Imagine if we were closer to the sun, and I mean much closer, closer than any of the planets in our solar system, its heat and radiation would kill us. God's holiness can be likened to the intensity of the sun, but even the sun as a created object falls short of the intensity of God's holiness. As a result, in order that man might walk in the presence of God again, he had to be made right again. Man's sin had to be dealt with. In his book, *On the Incarnation*, Athanasius writes that:

> ...only the assumption of humanity by one who is himself fully divine could effect a change in this creaturely state; by becoming human and living a human life, the divine Word, who is in himself the true image of God, restored the image of God that is marred in us.[15]

If Christ were to be less than God in his essence, then salvation would be impossible, because no created creature could possibly deliver us from our fallen condition and bring us into life and right standing with God. Only someone equal to God can be man's saviour, and not only equal but same in substance, for God's word teaches us that there is only one true God. This is what Jesus meant by claiming to be the way, the truth and the life. He sets the parameters by which we might understand the world, furnishing us with a true philosophy of life, and calling us to respond to the truth.

---

15. Cited in Ivor J. Davidson, *A Public Faith: From Constantine to the Medieval World AD 312-600*, ed. John D. Woodbridge, David F. Wright, and Tim Dowley, Volume Two (Grand Rapids, MI.: Baker Books, 2005), 64.

How do we now then compare the person of Christ and his teachings to other religious worldviews?

2.5 Comparing Jesus with other Religious Figures

Those who often object to Christ's exclusive claims and label him as potentially "intolerant" or "disrespectful towards other religions" echo the common train of thought of the Eastern religions, principally, that of "relativism." Given the limited amount of time I have, I am unfortunately forced to limit myself to selecting only two religious worldviews that are the most representative of the Eastern religions. These are Hinduism and Buddhism, the former emerging first, and the latter developing from later Hinduism. While there are other Eastern religions to consider, such Shintoism, Jainism, and Bahaism to name a few, the underlying principle remains the same, the blurring of the Creator-creation distinction. I will address this matter as we move forward.

Firstly, however, it needs to be said that, in the Eastern religions, there is no such thing as "absolute truth," and this is because truth is considered relative. Truth can have various meanings, even opposites that contradict. You can be god, and not god. You can be real, and not real. You can be conscious, and not conscious. So the claims of Christ, as he meant them, are not generally accepted as they are, but rather reinterpreted to fit within the Eastern worldview, and for this reason he is often venerated as one of many gods, or as a *bodhisattva* (a Buddha in the making). I intend to return to the matter of the nature of truth in Eastern thinking, but let us first deconstruct the core essence of both the Hindu and Buddhist worldviews.

2.5.1 Hinduism

As it concerns Hinduism, the religious worldview underwent three phases of religious development. These phases are respectively called the *Vedic* phase, the *Vedantic* phase, and the *Bhakti* phase.[16] The *Vedic* phase is believed to have begun sometime around 1500 BC, and was characterized by ritual and legal requirements that were administered by the priesthood of the Brahmins. Each member of the caste system had to fulfill their religious duty in order to escape the endless cycle of reincarnation, and for most this meant that only the highest caste (which were the Brahmins) were closer to escaping *samsara* (reincarnation). This elitist framework of religious practice led to later revolts and reforms by the lower castes, leading to the *Vedantic* phase of 500 BC.[17]

This second phase was characterized by various forms of withdrawal, meditation, and yoga, which, as opposed to the first phase, could be practiced by all caste members. The objective of these mystical practices was to arrive at the true realization of the *Atman-Brahman* identity. What this means is to recognize one's own personal identity as an illusion, because we are nothing more than extensions of the impersonal

---

16. Winfried Corduan, *Neighboring Faiths: A Christian Introduction to World Religions*, Second ed. (Downers Grove, IL.: IVP Academic, 2012), 268.

17. Ibid.

god *Brahman*. Achieving this realization would supposedly open the door to escaping the cycle of reincarnation, and allow the soul to reunite with the oneness of the universe, *Brahman*.

Brahman is the impersonal god of Hinduism. It is not a person, it is not an individual. It is quite simply pantheistic, all-pervasive, sometimes referred to as the "world soul."[18] To further simplify this for you: pantheism is the concept of "god is all, and all is god." So, for the Hindu, "Brahman is all, and all is Brahman." This philosophy is regarded as the *Advaita Vedanta*, in which *Advaita* means "non-dual." In other words, there is no distinction or division between different aspects of reality, all is one. And yet, the term "one" is not appropriate, because as a number it is different from the numbers two, three, and four, etc. In essence, there can be no such distinctions within *Advaita*.

This mystical phase of Hinduism is referred to as the "way of knowledge" (*jnana-marga*), a freedom from the illusion of *maya*, which is the magical play of *Brahman*, and an attainment of the knowledge of reality.[19] In other words, the intellectual, psychological and religious faculties of man are not really extensions of *Brahman*'s impersonal entity, but rather playful manifestations. Like a puppeteer, whose hand is in the puppet. The puppeteer can make the puppet laugh, shout, and move about, but we all know the puppet is not really autonomous. Instead, the human hand inside the puppet is moving the puppet to act and communicate. In

18. Ibid., 280.
19. Ibid.

the same way, our emotions, intellect and behaviour are supposedly the coordinated play of *Brahman*, but it is not *Brahman* itself, it is an illusion. It is *maya*, the word associated with "magic." As the religion scholar Dr. Winfried Corduan writes:

> We may think of *maya* as the image created by a movie projector or as a dream: experientially real but insubstantial. If we immerse ourselves in the projection or the dream as genuine reality, we will live in ignorance (*avidya*), and this state will keep us from finding true reality and thus keep us confined to the cycle of *samsara*.[20]

In other words, that which is *Brahman* is real, and that which is not *Brahman* is merely *maya*, an illusion, the magical play (*lila*) arising from *Brahman*. Only by seeing the illusion, and the real behind the illusion, can one escape reincarnation. But this was not the only means of the Hindu's salvation.

The later phase of *Bhakti* emerged with the text of the *Bhagavad-Gita* some time around 200 BC. It is regarded by Hindus as a sacred book, and for non-Hindus as a literary epic. In the *Bhagavad-Gita* we read of the story of Arjuna, a heroic archer, and his conflict with his cousins, the Kauravas. The story is centered around Arjuna's moral dilemma as to whether he should fulfill his duty as a warrior (and as part of the warrior caste), or to be slain so that he would not shed his family's blood. This moral dilemma is worked out through a conversation with his charioteer, Krishna, who is supposedly the Hindu god *Vishnu* in human flesh.

---

20. Ibid.

We will return to the *Bhagavad-Gita* momentarily, but for now it is enough to say that the text portrays the personal devotion towards a god as sufficient grounds by which man can escape the cycle of reincarnation. This is what the term *Bhakti* means, the way of devotion (*bhakti-marga*).[21]

Contemporary Hinduism is a by-product of these three historical phases, but at its core it has always maintained the following: The impersonal god *Brahman* is all things, and all things is the impersonal god *Brahman*. This is a complete oneness without any distinctions, and any perceived distinctions within the universe are merely *maya*, the playful illusions of *Brahman*.

This is the underlying principle of all Eastern religions. In the case of the Hindu worldview, there is no distinction between Creator and creation, there is no dualism according to the philosophy of *Advaita Vedanta*, all is one. The term that might be used to describe this lack of distinction is *One-ism*. It is a term coined by the scholar Peter Jones, author of the book *One or Two: Seeing a World of Difference*. The concept, however, is not novel, but rather is rooted in the New Testament (Rom. 1). The apostle Paul divides humanity into two groups: those who rightly worship the Creator as wholly distinct from creation (*Two-ism*), and those who wrongly worship and deify the creation (*One-ism*). Hinduism falls under the latter.

The One-ist worldview affirms the following, either explicitly or implicitly:[22]

---

21. Ibid., 281.
22. For more on Oneism and Twoism, see Peter Jones, *One or*

1. **All is One** and everything is divine (there is no external god; and spirituality is in ourselves and in the universe around us);

2. **Humanity is One** and everyone shares in the divine power (if we all unite, we can bring the world to a new level of happiness and peace);

3. **Religions are One** and each religion has some of the truth (if we bring them all together, we will discover real spirituality – the main thrust of religious pluralism in the West);

4. The **problem** with mankind is that we must remember that we are one (distinctions such as black and white keep us from true unity and spirituality);

5. The **solution** is that we look within ourselves to find power and unifying balance (we become spiritual as we experience the unity of all things and lose ourselves in the all).

This is, essentially, a form of religious humanism, because at its core, man is deified. There may be millions of gods within the Hindu pantheon, and they may all be superior in strength and power to man, but they too are merely extensions of the impersonal god *Brahman*. This means that, according to Hinduism, we are little gods as well. As a former Catholic who converted to Hinduism said: "Whereas Christianity says: Repent, you're a Sinner; Hinduism says: Awaken!

Two: Seeing a World of Difference (Escondido, CA.: Main Entry Editions, 2010).

You're Divine!"[23]

Now, there are obvious problems with a pantheistic, One-ist worldview like Hinduism. First of all, the pre-conditions for intelligibility are lost. Or to put it more plainly, the laws of logic and reason that are used to explain the Hindu religion are lost, because there are no absolutes in a world that is simply one impersonal god with no distinctions. There are no true and false, no right and wrong, no light and darkness, no male and female. There are NO distinctions, and within such a worldview, everything breaks down. Communication is no longer possible, information in any form is no longer information, just raw data of "sameness" which bears no meaning. This is why the human being has no value. This is why the soul is no different than your dog, or your cat, or the cockroach living in your home.

The implications can go even further. There are no distinctions between living beings and non-living things. No difference between a man and a rock, because they are essentially extensions of the same *Brahman*. A person could pour boiling water on his neighbour without repercussion because it is merely *Brahman* being poured out by *Brahman* on *Brahman*. This inevitably leads to moral chaos, it undermines the foundations of human rights and liberty, and even contradicts the Hindu caste system and the concept of *karma*.

We can consult the *Bhagavad-Gita*, which illustrates the moral breakdown of a One-ist worldview. In the

23. Ma Nithya Swarupapriyananda, "Difference between Christianity & Hinduism: Repent, you're a sinner vs. Awaken! You're divine!", *Youtube*. Accessed January 31, 2016, https://www.youtube.com/watch?v=x5gARFv4wrk.

beginning of the book, Arjuna states:

> I foresee no good resulting from slaughtering my kin
> in war!... What joy for us in murdering [the Kauravas],
> O Krishna? For if we killed these murderers, evil like
> theirs would cling to us!... Even if they, mastered by
> greed, are blind to the consequences of the family's de-
> struction, of friendships lost to treachery, how are we
> not to comprehend that we must turn back from evil?[24]

Arjuna struggles with the "old man" of the sinner, what the Christian theologian Cornelius Van Til refers to as man's original state of righteousness prior to the fall. He recognizes that to take a life is evil, and that it would be better to be slain than to commit murder against his own family. It is in his discourse that he unveils the human condition which the Bible adequately describes (cf. Gen. 6:5): "It grieves me that as we intend to murder our relatives in our greed for pleasures, kingdoms, we are fixed on doing evil!"[25]

At this point in time, *Krishna*, the charioteer, is not yet revealed to be the god *Vishnu* incarnated, and in his dialogue in the *Bhagavad-Gita*, he counsels Arjuna as to what is important: (1) To fulfill one's duty, and in doing so, to be (2) indifferent as to whether an action is moral or immoral. In other words, the question of right and wrong is not important, morality is not necessary when it conflicts with the duty to fulfill and adhere to the

---

24. *The Bhagavad Gita: A New Translation*, A New Translation, trans. Gavin Flood and Charles Martin (New York, NY.: W.W. Norton & Company, 2012), 6-9.

25. Ibid., 9.

caste system and its function in society.

It is in the eleventh chapter where *Krishna* finally unveils his true nature, seeing that only by the authority of a god can Arjuna be persuaded to take up arms. The pantheism of Hinduism is evident in this moment of revelation, as Krishna in all his glory reveals himself as the god *Vishnu* in human flesh: "Here behold all the universe, beings moving and motionless, standing as one in my body, and all else that you wish to see!"[26]

Arjuna must learn to be indifferent, and to carry out his caste's obligation as a warrior, not caring whether he causes pleasure or pain.[27] As a One-ist worldview, where there is no Creator-creation distinction, but rather a combination of both divine and infinite with the finite and temporal, there is an inevitable breakdown of reality, knowledge and morality. These are but some of the implications of Hinduism, the various systematic failures which render it false and impossible to abide by.

2.5.2 Buddhism

We could also turn to Buddhism and see how it too falls into *One-ism*. Prior to proceeding, however, I must make clear that Buddhism is not easily summarized. Corduan explains the difficulty: "...the distinctions between different schools of Buddhism are so stark that it becomes quite difficult to identify a basic core."[28] Nonetheless, a basic core can be found, if not in terms

---

26. Ibid., 90.
27. Corduan, *Neighboring Faiths*, 282.
28. Ibid., 313.

of practice, certainly in terms of thought. And what better way to mine this thought than by beginning with the teachings of the Buddha? In order to understand his teachings, however, we must first have an understanding of his origin.

According to Buddhist traditions, the Buddha was originally called Siddhartha Gautama, a Hindu prince of the Shakya clan. The father of Gautama was a king who desired greatness for his son's reign, and so, in an effort to preserve his being and character, he kept him away from religion, death, disease, old age, and other visible traits of the human condition. He would eventually take a wife named Yasodhara, who bore him a son, Rahula.[29]

Because of Gautama's persistence, his father granted him a trip outside of the royal palace. But before the journey took place, the king sent his soldiers to purge the area of his intended travel from all death, disease, and suffering. There are two versions to this story, the one from the Hindus is that the Hindu deities manifested themselves as an old man close to death, a man with leprosy, a funeral procession for a decomposed corpse, and a monk withdrawing from life. The Buddhist version of this story is that Gautama took a different turn than was planned and came across a village that was not purged by the king, and he witnessed all these things. In either case, what Gautama had seen provoked guilt and remorse because of his privileged position as prince. This guilt led him to abandon his

---

29. Ibid., 315-316.

position, his family, and his wealthy inheritance, fleeing in the night from the palace.

In an effort to alleviate his guilt, he deprived himself of human comforts and good health, and after seven years of poverty and self-inflicted harm, he decided to either succeed in his redemption or die from starvation. It was reportedly that, while he was under a fig tree during his meditation, he reached enlightenment and became the "awakened one."[30] He would, since then, teach others for decades as to how to reach enlightenment, for everyone sought to be free from their guilt and suffering. The popularity that followed Gautama would eventually pave the way for the Buddhist religion to develop and emerge. And it is claimed, by both Hindus and Buddhists, that on the day that Gautama had died from food poisoning, he had escaped the cycle of reincarnation and was united with Nirvana (*Brahman* for the Hindus).[31] There was, of course, no way of verifying this belief, but it became the pinnacle of hope for many in the East.

According to the teachings of the Buddha (which were later expanded in the Pali Canon), the world is ultimately impermanent. In other words, all of visible reality is an illusion, and this illusion is in a constant state of flux. As a result, no human being can hold on to something, even if that something was permanent, because all is an illusion. This causes great suffering, because we, who do not exist, cling to something that is temporary. The solution, according to Gautama, was

30. Ibid., 317.
31. Ibid., 318.

to internalize the truth of our non-existence, and by doing so we could escape the cycle of reincarnation and join Nirvana. Nirvana is a oneness that is often described as a nothingness, but which cannot be fully explained because it completely transcends human language. This is the Eastern version of atheism, discarding all gods as wishful thinking for the permanent, but as opposed to the rationalism and materialism that characterizes Western atheism, Buddhism instead prides itself with its irrationalism and mysticism.

In order to internalize the teachings of the Buddha, man must accept the four noble truths, that: (1) to live is to suffer; (2) suffering is caused by attachment; (3) to eliminate suffering one must eliminate attachment; and (4) one can eliminate attachment by following the eightfold path.[32]

The eightfold path consists of the following:

1. The Right View (understanding the illusion of reality);
2. The Right Intention (willing to achieve enlightenment);
3. The Right Speech (say what is required);
4. The Right Action (doing what is required);
5. The Right Livelihood (monkship);
6. The Right Effort (energy concentration);
7. The Right Mindfulness (meditation);
8. And Right Concentration (focus).[33]

---

32. Ibid., 320.
33. Ibid., 320-321.

But if everything is truly one, and all an illusion, how can we be certain about what the Buddha teaches? Is not Buddha himself an illusion? Is not his religious practice and teaching a manifestation of non-existence? If the only thing that is eternal is the nothingness of Nirvana, is it not contradictory to attach oneself to the four noble truths? Is not suffering caused by attachment? These are the questions we are forced to ask, and these were the kind of questions Buddha had to face.

In one of his dialogues concerning the summit of human consciousness, Gautama states that there is one summit and in the same sense there are several. As a result of this contradiction, his followers asked him whether this philosophy (or certain aspects of this philosophy) should be considered true and all others false. Gautama's response as the awakened one fails to satisfy the inquirer, as he says:

> [There is no] profit, it is not concerned with the Norm, it does not [relate to the eightfold path], it does not redound to real knowledge, nor to insight (of the higher stages of the Path), nor to Nirvana. Therefore is it that I express no opinion upon it.[34]

Essentially, in order to avoid the question of exclusivity, or to even avoid implying inclusivity, Gautama chooses to remain silent. For a "wise" teacher of the East, who supposedly reached enlightenment, this is an embarrassing statement. He refuses to make any truth

---

34. "IX. Potthapâda Sutta", *Sacred Texts*. Accessed April 6, 2016, http://www.sacred-texts.com/bud/dob/dob-09tx.htm.

claims, and he refuses to affirm his teaching as absolutely true. Why then consider his teachings? But then, this would be consistent with the Buddhist worldview. Is not all an illusion? Therefore his teachings are an illusion too. There can be no distinctions within a One-ist worldview in which all is one, a great vast nothingness, Nirvana. We should not expect, as a result, that the laws of logic apply, because outside of the biblical worldview, the laws of logic and reasoning cannot be satisfactorily justified. There is no way to make sense of logic and truth outside of the being of the biblical God who is the source for all forms of logic, and who is himself the truth.

2.5.3 Islam

Now at this point you may well be ready to say: "It is all very easy to dismiss the religions of the East, but what about the Western religions, like Islam? It is, after all, very similar to Christianity." Let me explain to you why Islam, which presents itself as a "Two-ist" worldview (preserving the Creator and creation distinction), is actually a "One-ist" worldview.

According to the Islamic doctrine of *tawhid*, Allah is an absolute unity. It is the unity and singularity of Allah's oneness that makes Islam, in the Muslim's mind, the "purest form of monotheism."[35] And given the doctrine of *tanzih*, in which creation is altogether separate from the Creator, there must therefore be a distinction between Creator and creation, which is vital

---

35. Alhaj A.D. Ajijola, *The Essence of Faith in Islam* (Lahore, Pakistan: Islamic Publications Ltd., 1978), 55.

for the comprehension of the intelligibility of human experience (philosophers call this the "predication of reality"). But if we examine the Qur'anic text, the Islamic traditions (the hadith), and the commentaries that followed, we will discover a dialectical tension between the absolute transcendence of Allah, and the sameness of Allah with all creation.

The commentators Shihab al-Din al-Alusi and Muhammad ibn Ali al-Shawkani claim that the Qur'an depicts Allah as "absolutely transcendent," bearing no likeness to creation whatsoever.[36] This is problematic, because to say anything about Allah theologically, or to even think and conceptualize Allah, is to deny his absolute transcendence and render him "knowable." According to Islam, this is the sin of *shirk*, the wrongful association of Allah with anything created. As the commentator Fadl Allah writes, "the mental faculty cannot reach Him in His elusive and hidden mystery."[37]

Allah is essentially unknowable, inapproachable, and unintelligible to the human mind. This is because there exists no possible likeness between Allah and creation, nothing to tether him to this world. If, therefore, nothing can truly be known about the Creator, then nothing can be known about creation, because to say

---

36. The commentaries of Shihab al-Din al-Alusi, *Ruh al-ma ani fi tafsir al-Qur'an al-azim wa'l-sab al-mathani* and Muhammad ibn Ali al-Shawkani, *Fath al-qadir* in Nasr et al., eds., *The Study Qur'an: A New Translation and Commentary* (New York, NY: Harper Collins Publishers, 2015), 1580.

37. Feras Hamza, Sajjad Rizvi, and Farhana Mayer, eds., *An Anthology of Qur'anic Commentaries*, Vol. 1 (London, UK. Oxford University Press, 2008), 492.

that creation reflects the Creator is ultimately *shirk*, the reduction of Allah from his pure transcendence. But interestingly, just as the Qur'anic text provides support for this "absolute transcendence," it also provides support for Allah's sameness with creation.

In spite of Allah's absolute transcendence, the Qur'an depicts Allah as the Willer of all things, and given the implied meaning of its supporting passages, Allah becomes "indistinguishable from 'nature' and 'fate' itself, because everything becomes an expression of pure will."[38] In other words, because nothing exists outside of Allah's will, because nothing happens without it being an extension of Allah, as per Al-Ghazali, then Allah is all things. As he himself wrote:

> Indeed there is nothing in existence except God and His acts, for whatever is there besides Him is His act…. [mystics] are able to see visually that there is no being in the world other than God and that the face of everything is perishable save His face (S. 28:88) … indeed, everything other than He, considered in itself, is pure non-being …therefore, nothing is except God Almighty and His face.[39]

This is why, no matter where you are or where you might turn, there you find "the Face of Allah" (S.

---

38. Joseph Boot, "Nature & Revelation: The Fractured Foundations of Islam," in *Jubilee: Recovering Biblical Foundations for our Time*, ed. Ryan Eras, Summer 2016 (Toronto: Ezra Institute for Contemporary Christianity), 11.

39. Al-Ghazali, cited in Robert R. Reilly, *The Closing of the Muslim Mind: How Intellectual Suicide Created the Modern Islamist Crisis* (Wilmington, DE.: ISI Books, 2010), 110.

2:115).[40] All things other than Allah are non-being, so therefore, all of created reality must be Allah.

This pantheistic claim would be quickly debated by any Muslim, but Al-Ghazali's written words articulate the thought of early Muslims and the progress of Qur'anic interpretation. Islam is, therefore, an awkward synthesis of "pure monotheism" and "pantheism," running into problems on both ends. For Allah to be absolutely transcendent renders all created reality unknowable, and for Allah to be one with everything is to render reality unintelligible. Islam attempts to copy the Christian worldview as "Two-ist", but fails to exhibit the distinction between Creator and creation, and thus is "One-ist" by implication. Had Mohammed either known or accepted the fact that his Qur'an was in conflict with the Torah (*Taurat*) and the Gospel (*Injil*), which the Qur'an regards as authorities above itself (S. 10:94), Islam would have never developed. Though the Qur'an may make similar claims to that of the Bible, upon verifying its claims, it falls flat on its face, exhibiting its various internal inconsistencies.

2.6 The Only Two-ist Worldview

In the end, as we compare these three religious worldviews, Hinduism, Buddhism and Islam – which, in

---

40. The scholastic Ghazalian names of Allah are interpreted as a "network of hierarchal manifestations or epiphanies of the Divine Essence through which the mystic progressed to be united with the Being of God" in Ahad M. Ahmed, "The Theological Thought of Fazlur Rahman: A Modern Mutakkalim", *Archive*. Accessed January 9, 2017, https://archive.org/stream/thetheologicalthoughtoffazlurrahman-thesisbyahadmaqboolahmed/the-theological-thought-of-fazlur-rahman-thesis-by-ahad-maqbool-ahmed_djvu.txt/.

terms of their internal inconsistencies, are representative of other world religions – and as we consider the claims of Christ and the worldview from which his claims are made, it is only according to the presuppositions of God's word, the Bible, that we are able to make sense of reality.

The Christian worldview corresponds to reality, it coheres, its consistent, it exhibits the distinction between Creator and creation, and as such we can make sense of the distinctions, the intelligibility and the meaningfulness of the human experience. To put it quite simply, the claims of Christ, and therefore of Christianity, are *absolutely true because of the impossibility of the contrary*.

Christ is God incarnate, and given the impossibility of other religious worldviews, he is undeniably the way, the truth and the life. He claimed to be so, and we can take him for his word and verify that it is so. As Van Til wrote:

> Now in fact, I feel that the whole of history and civilization would be unintelligible to me if it were not for my belief in God. So true is this, that I propose to argue that unless God is back of everything, you cannot find meaning in anything.[41]

Krishna (who did not historically exist), Siddhartha Gautama (who is thought to be a myth), Muhammad (who cannot be confirmed historically[42]), and all

---

41. Cornelius Van Til, *Why I Believe in God* (Philadelphia: Committee on Christian Education of the Orthodox Presbyterian Church, n.d.), 3.

42. See Robert Spencer, *Did Muhammad Exist? An Inquiry into*

other religious figures, cannot compare to the radiant uniqueness and reality of Jesus Christ and what he means for our fallen world. Christ is the way of salvation and redemption, the standard bearer of truth, and the life-giver and restorer. No one can come to the Father except through him, and to know him is to know the Father.

And that says something about religious pluralism. It means that no synthesis, no supplementation, no mingling can be possible between truth and error. This is significant, because as the World Parliament of Religions continues to assemble for the application of religion to society (in 2018 it will have taken place in my city of Toronto), no true culture will ever emerge from a syncretized religion. And by "true culture," I mean a culture that is rooted structurally in God's law-word and directed toward him in rightful, vertical worship, this is the practice of true religion.

Whether it is an Islamic culture, a Hindu culture, a secular humanistic culture, a religious pluralistic culture, there are only two worldviews underlying culture, and these two conflict with each other: it is the One-ist worldview of creation-worship, and the Two-ist worldview of Creator-worship. This makes all culture, by implication, religious, because it is the cultivation of creation according to the prevailing *cultus* (Latin for "worship") of the people. And as we can derive, a "One-ist" worldview that cannot make sense of reality cannot contribute meaningfully towards human prog-

---

Islam's Obscure Origins (Delaware Intercollegiate Studies Institute, 2012).

ress. How can it when it cannot provide standards for justice, ethics, economics, etc. if all is one and undifferentiated?

Since culture is the result of man's beneficial interaction with God's creation, and since man is a religious being by nature, then whatever culture man may cultivate will be religious in nature as well. And it follows that, as there is a thing as true worship, in terms of God's word and law-order, and true worldview, then there must also be true culture, a culture that is consistent with the teaching of God's word both structurally and directionally. It is the only culture in which man may realize his true calling, cultivating true progress toward realizing God's perfect standards on earth. This is what the Bible means by the righteous living *by faith* (Rom. 1:17), an all-inclusive and comprehensive "living" that concerns the just governance of Jesus Christ over all things.

This is the gospel that the apostles proclaimed, the redemption and recovery of man's true purpose in Jesus Christ to cultivate God's creation into a godly civilization, to build His kingdom on earth by the proclamation of the truth and the administering of His grace, as all things are brought subject to the Lordship of Christ who reigns over heaven and earth (1 Cor. 15:25-28).

Can Man Live Without God?

"I have seen everything that is done under the sun, and behold, all is vanity and a striving after wind."

– Ecclesiastes 1:14

3.1 Introduction

IN THE PAST FEW YEARS, I have had the privilege of traveling and speaking in different parts of the Americas and the Caribbean, and wherever I have gone I have been reminded time and again of perhaps the greatest question of our time: Can man live without God? The popular historian and philosopher, Will Durant, attempted to answer this in his book, *On the Meaning of Life*. He describes that in the Fall of 1930, he found himself in Lake Hill, New York, raking leaves. He was approached at the time by a well-dressed man who told him in a quiet tone that he was going to kill himself unless the philosopher could give him a valid reason not to. Durant did the best he possibly could to answer his questions, and the fate of that stranger was left a mystery. But haunted by this experience he contacted various experts on arts, politics, religion, and the sciences, to help him provide a response to the fundamental question of life's meaning. There responses formed the book *On the Meaning of Life.*

The apologist Ravi Zacharias writes in relation to the question that:

> ...philosophizing on life's purpose is ultimately founded upon two fundamental assumptions, or conclusions. The first is, Does God exist? And the second, If God exists, what is His character or nature? The questions are impossible to ignore, and if they are not dealt with formally, their implications filter down into everyday life. It is out of one's belief or disbelief in God that all other convictions are formed.[1]

As human beings, we are by nature inquisitive about our reality, and we have every right to ask questions about our world. We walk daily under the sun, engaging in various activities, studies, and disciplines, but always asking if there is a point to all that we do. How do make sense of our world? What makes our human experience meaningful? We have several questions concerning who we are, our place in the world, and what we were meant to be and do. But just as we are ready to ask these questions, we must ask ourselves, would we be willing to submit to the truth, even if it runs contrary to what we earnestly *desire* to be true?

---

1.   Ravi Zacharias, *Can Man Live Without God?* (Nashville, TN.: W Publishing Group, 1994), 8.

3.2 Man's Desire to be Free

To comprehend what is being asked by the question "Can Man Live Without God?", we must first address which God we are referring to. Are we speaking about the Greek gods like Zeus, Poseidon and Aphrodite? Are we speaking about the god of Islam, or the Brahma of Hinduism?

When I am asked this question, it is not the gods of ancient Greece or Rome that are under the spotlight. It is not any of the pantheistic gods of the East. It is not any of the animistic spirits of the indigenous. The question is referring to the God of Christian theism, whose written revelation in the Bible has helped steer Western civilization towards progress and the betterment of society. So we ought to phrase the question this way: "Can man live without the *biblical* God?"

Having now clarified *which* God we are talking about (the one and only true God), we also need to consider from what worldview this question is coming from. I had previously defined the term *worldview* in my last lecture, allow me to summarize what the term means by citing the scholar John Frame, who writes: "a worldview is a general conception of the universe."[2] It is what you believe to be true, it is what you believe about reality, about knowledge, about ethics. Every element of human experience is thus interpreted by your own worldview.

There is a vast diversity of worldviews in the West,

---

2.   John M. Frame, *A History of Western Philosophy and Theology* (Phillipsburg, NJ.: P&R Publishing, 2015), 1.

but the undercurrent that has linked these worldviews together is the philosophy of rationalism and secularism. In recent years, man has reduced "religion" (most particularly Christianity) to an imaginary private sphere by artificially separating it from the public sphere. And this separation essentially says that God has no say on matters of public life, for this is the realm of "reason." Now, there is no doubt that other religions have enjoyed more daylight in the public square than Christianity in recent years, but this is because all non-Christian worldviews have a common trait, they are humanistic at their core, which means that man is regarded, whether explicitly or implicitly, as the measure of all things. But the implications of absolutizing reason, and removing God, prompted the great question of our time: Can man live without God? It has become apparent that, without God, we can know nothing of the meaningfulness of human experience, or of the intelligibility of reality. We are left just as hopeless as that man in Lake Hill, New York, desperately searching for a reason to go on.

The question itself, "Can man live without God?" is an accurate depiction of man's historical struggle to live, think and believe rightly. We cannot divorce this question from its history of human thought, especially when we consider that the West was largely developed by the Christian worldview prior to Enlightenment and Romanticist philosophy. As Christian thinker Joe Boot writes in his book *The Mission of God*: "It is simply not possible to account for the liberty created by Western civilization without recognizing the specifically Christian and biblical faith that forms its actuating principle."[3] The development of Western civilization was, after all, built on the bedrock of Christian theism.

What we are presently witnessing in the Western world, however, is the continued departure from our Christian-religious roots. And the further we have strayed, the louder the question has become, the unforeseen result of adopting the principles of Enlightenment thought. The Enlightenment can be defined as that rationalistic, intellectual movement of the 18th century, where man sought "to dominate by reason, a series of human problems in the world, and in particular, its fight for liberty, progress and equality,"[4] and it had a profound influence on Western culture. It was not that the Christian faith could not provide the foundation for liberty, progress and equality (for it had already done so – as for example depicted in the life of William Wilberforce and his abolition of the slave trade), but rather that man sought to realize such things independently from the God of Christian theism.

Natural man thought to himself that true liberty, progress and equality had to be free from the governance of God, and thus philosophers like Voltaire (1694-1778) and Thomas Paine (1737-1809) emerged amongst the many as advocates for a radical human-

3. Joseph Boot, *The Mission of God: A Manifesto of Hope for Society*, Kindle Edition (Toronto, ON.: Ezra Press, 2016), Loc. 2138.

4. Jaime Jaramillo Uribe, *Nueva Historia de Colombia, Tomo 2: Republica Sigo XIX*, ed. Camilo Calderon Schrader (Bogota, Colombia: Planeta Colombiana Editorial S.A., 1989), 11.

ism. Voltaire, for example, believed that the first step towards human progress involved casting off biblical authority and purging society from all Christian influence.[5] Thomas Paine, author of *The Age of Reason*, believed in the "natural rights of mankind" and the "influence of reason and principle" over and above Scripture.[6] Their voices are joined by a whole throng of rationalists who believed that knowledge about reality can be acquired independently of God, and thus there exists no need for man to live in communion with God.

Since then, secularism has gripped the West with an iron vice in an attempt to interpret our world, and to govern it, independently from "religion." One might say that it is the attempt for man to live, think and believe *neutrally*, all while avoiding the controversy associated with religion. This can be depicted by the secularist's "two-storey" analogy, where a house of two floors is divided into two different levels. The lower-storey, according to educator Mark L. Ward, "is where most Western people put the science, math, and the facts," information that we "think" we can know with certainty.[7] While everything else like religion, morals and aesthetics can go in the upper-storey, supposedly things we cannot know for certain.

5. See Voltaire, *Oeuvres Complètes de Voltaire*, Vol. 7, ed. Georges Avenel (Paris: Aux Bureaux du Siècle, 1869).

6. See Thomas Paine, *The Age of Reason*, Complete Edition (USA: World Union of Deists, 2013).

7. Mark L. Ward, ed., *Biblical Worldview: Creation, Fall, Redemption* (Greenville, SC.: BJU Press, 2016), 34-35.

In the lower-storey, we have the public sphere, we have the "facts" which are binding on everyone, and everything is "rational." While in the upper-storey we have the private sphere, such as personal preferences, values which are determined by individual choice, and all other things that are not deemed rational (including the spiritual). How might this play out in reality?

Suppose you are presenting an argument before national Parliament. The debate happens to be about the potential criminalization of pornography, and your argument, with evidence in hand, is that "both men and women should have no access to pornography because it is associated with domestic violence, sexual assault, and human trafficking." Though not everyone might agree with you, they will nonetheless see this as an appropriate argument. Why? Because you are reasoning based on the correlations you are deducing from available research statistics.

But if you were to argue that "pornography is wrong because God's word says fornication and adultery are wrong," this would not be considered acceptable. Depending on the country's cultural composition, you might be silenced, laughed out of Parliament, or even black-listed. But there was a time in the West where Judaeo-Christian morality was outright acknowledged. For example, in a 1906 Senate debate in Canada, a Liberal Senator named James McMullen asked, in regards to the Ten Commandments, why all the commandments were confirmed by national legislation and not that of the Sabbath. He even directly quoted Scripture in his argument, what would have been deemed unacceptable in our day and age.[8]

A lot has changed since then, however. Given the two-storey view which has developed throughout Western society, the moment you speak on the authority of God's word (the Bible), as Ward puts it: "you'll be escorted up the stairs to the second-storey and told that you have to quit trying to impose your religion on the rational, scientifically verifiable facts downstairs in the living room."[9] In other words, "keep your faith in the private sphere," do not let it enter the public sphere, because it is not a public "fact."

What might be considered the *public* sphere? The term itself refers to "all the many places (books, magazines, the internet, city halls, courtrooms, Parliament, etc.) where issues are debated publicly."[10] Following this line of thinking, man might live with God if he wants to, just as long as he stays in the upper-storey. Why? Because God has no place in the lower-storey of reality. That itself would be "neutral" ground. But to think that such ground is irreligious is absurd when we consider that no human being can possibly separate his beliefs, values and morality from the public sphere. We are, by nature, religious beings, and therefore all that we examine in the sciences, all that we examine in academia, all that we decide in law-making, will be shaped and interpreted by our own religious worldview. The

---

8. See Michael Wagner, *Leaving God Behind: The Charter of Rights and Canada's Official Rejection of Christianity* (Russell, Ontario: Christian Governance, 2012), 25.

9. Ward, ed., *Biblical Worldview*, 35.

10. Ibid.

two-storey analogy is thus false and impossible to realize.

Secularism, therefore, is not an elimination of religion from the public sphere, but rather the substitution
of the Christian religion with some form of humanism,
where man can be his own creator, governor, deliverer
and sustainer of all things. He can be his own "god",
as Adam and Eve wrongfully sought in the Garden
of Eden. He now attempts to do this while under the
veil of "secularism" or "neutrality", a clear betrayal of
what he initially sought to propagate. As Boot writes:

> We must begin by recognizing the fact that no culture
> can be neutral. It is impossible for any social order to
> be neutral – that is, neither one thing nor another. Ev-
> ery civilization is and will be inescapably committed,
> through the spheres and institutions of family, acade-
> my, law, art and government, to a religious or cultural
> consensus, be it humanistic, Islamic, Hindu, Christian
> or any other. The illusory idea of a neutral order or
> *prejudice-free* space for an equal toleration of all views (or
> gods) is a myth utilized only to facilitate the establish-
> ment of a new intolerance.[11]

I have grown to greatly appreciate the work of
Greg L. Bahnsen in this area of exposing the myth of
neutrality. In his book, *Pushing the Antithesis*, he provides
two examples as to how it is absolutely impossible to
be neutral in public life. He writes of a college profes-
sor who, as an atheist, cleverly decides "which options
are serious, which questions are worthwhile, and what

---

11. Boot, *The Mission of God*, Loc. 6837.

evidence should be put before his class."[12] He even selects the reading assignments that align with his own worldview, all while leaving out Christian principles. Now for a supposedly "neutral" setting, the University, or the school at any level, is not very neutral at all.

Bahnsen also cites the supposed "neutral" tolerance of our Western society, where supposedly the government, the university and the media urge equal tolerance for all views, and particularly the "application of the neutrality principle to moral issues." But even in the midst of all this, the Christian view is rarely given equal tolerance. This is because, in our current culture, this so called "tolerance" is "intolerant of views that do not tolerate such things as homosexual conduct or feminism or abortion."[13]

Essentially, religious neutrality is a false reality (quite the conundrum), an illusion, just another attempt at man trying to escape from the reality of God. It is what apologists call the "myth" or "hypocrisy of neutrality."

Here, then, is my answer to the question Can man live without God?:

> *"Show me that he can... Show me that man can in fact live without God."*

3.3 The Inevitable Nihilistic Dilemma

Perhaps that takes you by surprise. Well, let me explain the rationale behind my answer. I believe that if God is

---

12. Greg L. Bahnsen, *Pushing the Antithesis: The Apologetic Methodology of Greg L. Bahnsen*, ed. Gary DeMar (Powder Springs, GA.: American Vision Press, 2007), 11.

13. Ibid., 11-12.

not the back of everything, then not only can man not live, he cannot even exist. To deny the God of Christian theism ultimately means that all of reality would cease to be intelligible, it would be void of meaning, rendering us incapable of giving an account of anything.

What I intend to make clear is that (i) the proof of the Christian worldview is found in the impossibility of the contrary, and (ii) that it is only from the Christian worldview that we can make sense of the intelligibility and meaningfulness of reality.

That is a bold statement. But let us say, for the sake of argument, that man can somehow rid himself of God, that with his "magic" eraser he was able to remove the God of Christian theism from reality. What would this mean for him and the world in which he lives? Someone has already answered that question. In spite of his hostility towards the Christian faith, the German philosopher Friedrich Nietzsche (1844-1900) rightly perceived the problem of "killing" God. He depicts this in his parable *The Madman*, in which he writes:

Whither is God? He cried;
> 'I will tell you. We have killed him – you and I.
> All of us are his murderers.
> But how did we do this?
> How could we drink up the sea?
> Who gave us the sponge to wipe away the entire horizon?
> What were we doing when we unchained this earth from its sun?
> Whither is it moving now?

Whither are we moving?
Away from all suns?
Are we not plunging continually?
Backward, sideward, forward, in all directions?
Is there still any up or down?
Are we not straying as through an infinite
nothing?
Do we not feel the breadth of empty space?
Has it not become colder?
Is not night continually closing in on us?
Do we not need to light lanterns in the morning?
Do we hear nothing as yet of the noise of the
gravediggers who are burying God?
Do we smell nothing as yet of the divine
decomposition?
Gods, too, decompose. God is dead. God remains
dead.
And we have killed him.[14]

I'm not sure if you have seen the meme that millennials have been circulating on social media lately, it is a meme in which Nietzsche's declaration that "God is dead" is comedically responded to by God saying "Nietzsche is dead" on the date of his passing. While the meme is meant to be comedic, it is actually quite tragic, Nietzsche never came to believe in the true God of Christian theism. What he believed – and this he believed rightly – was that to eliminate God, the giver of life, is to eliminate the distinction between the living and non-living. Consider this fact: Without God, we

14. Friedrich Nietzsche, *The Gay Science*, trans. Walter Kaufmann (Mineola, NY.: Dover Publications Inc., 2006), 90.

can know nothing about what is up and down, what is hot and cold, and what is real and the non-real. As Nietzsche said, are we not "straying as through an infinite nothing?"

Let me explain to you exactly what I mean. If we were to adopt the atheistic worldview, for example, which believes that the universe and the life within it is the cause of random natural processes, we would have to follow it through consistently as it relates to all areas of life. Let us start with the most basic observations, such as the laws of nature, the laws of physics, the laws of mathematics, etc. We would all agree that such things can be observed in our material universe. In fact, we are able to study our world because it behaves in an orderly manner that is intelligible and even predictable to us. If I drop an apple, it will fall. The same thing will happen if I drop a feather. We would be quite surprised if it suddenly began to float out into outer space, defying the law of gravity. In this we acknowledge that there is such a thing as gravity and that it follows certain rules. But how does the atheist justify this? That is to say, how does he make sense of this? In a universe that is governed by random chance, which is by its very nature always in flux, how can order result from chaos? How can laws, which are absolute, exist within a universe that is always changing and cannot tolerate absolute "fixed" laws? There is no way of justifying this from the atheistic perspective.

Instead of order we should have disorder. Instead of laws we should have random events that follow no discernible pattern or structure. Essentially, with the break down of all fixed rules and laws, the universe and all within it, down to the smallest micro-organism and the simplest human conversation, would be unintelligible. Just random and raw undifferentiated data with no discernible meaning.

So when we speak about observational science, when we speak about evidences and facts, we are only able to do so by presupposing the God of Christian theism who created our world and made us in his image. When the atheist, or the skeptic, attempts to use anything in our material world to mount an argument against God's existence, he is essentially using God's evidences, or God's facts, which have been grossly misinterpreted, because we are living in God's world. It is much the case as what the apologist Cornelius Van Til writes, "A little child may slap his father in the face, but he can do so only because the father holds him on his knee."[15]

But one might argue: "Very well, the atheistic worldview fails. But what about the other religious worldviews? Why does it have to be the Christian God and no other?" Because the other worldviews have much the same problem, they cannot make sense of our reality, they cannot give an intelligible account of anything. We have already taken a look at some of these religious worldviews in our previous lecture, but let us briefly review some of these, such as Hinduism.

According to the Hindu worldview, all is *Brahman*, and *Brahman* is all. In simpler terms, all is one with the

---

15. Cornelius Van Til, *The Case for Calvinism* (Phillipsburg, NJ.: P&R Publishing, 1979), 147-148.

impersonal god, and the impersonal god is all. This means that all the deities within Hinduism are merely extensions of this impersonal god. It is no secret that Hinduism is, essentially, a pantheistic religion. But herein lies the problem. There is no Creator-creation distinction, instead, Creator and creation are one. This means, by implication, that there can then be no distinctions within creation itself because it is part of the pure oneness, the "world soul." Good and evil are the same, up and down are the same, the words "you" and "me" are the same. If we are consistent with the pantheist worldview, then eliminating all distinctions reduces reality to undifferentiated oneness. Language would have no meaning because words could not have different meanings. Laws could not exist because what they prescribe and what they prohibit are much the same. The sun, the moon, the stars, even the lifeless materials like rocks are much the same as the living and breathing human being. Hinduism, and any other pantheistic worldview, can provide no intelligible account of reality.

What about Islam? If you recall, according to the doctrine of *tawhid*, Allah is an absolute unity. It is the unity and singularity of Allah's oneness that makes Islam, in the Muslim's mind, the "purest form of monotheism."[16] And given the doctrine of *tanzih*, in which creation is altogether separate from the Creator, there must then exist a Creator-creation distinction which is so vital to being able to make sense of reality. But

---

16. Alhaj A.D. Ajijola, *The Essence of Faith in Islam* (Lahore, Pakistan: Islamic Publications Ltd., 1978), 55.

one must examine this critically, because according to various Islamic commentators, Allah is depicted in the Qur'an as "absolutely transcendent," not bearing any likeness with creation.[17] Why is this a problem? Because to say anything about Allah theologically, or to even think and conceptualize Allah, is to render him "knowable," which according to Islam is *shirk*, the wrong (blasphemous) association of him with anything else. As the commentator Fadl Allah writes, "the mental faculty cannot reach Him in His elusive and hidden mystery."[18] Allah is essentially unknowable, inapproachable, unintelligible to the human mind, because there ultimately exists no possible likeness between him and creation. If, therefore, nothing can truly be known about the Creator, then nothing can be known about creation, because to say that creation reflects the Creator is ultimately *shirk*. The Islamic worldview, therefore, cannot make sense of reality because of its internal logical inconsistencies.

Also remember that I had earlier said that all worldviews, aside from Christianity, have no Creator-creation distinction. Islam is no exception. Despite of Allah's pure transcendence, the Qur'an describes Allah as the Willer of all things, and as a result becomes "indistinguishable from 'nature' and 'fate' itself, because

17. The commentaries of Shihab al-Din al-Alusi, *Ruh al-ma ani fi tafsir al-Qur'an al-azim wa'l-sab al-mathani* and Muhammad ibn Ali al-Shawkani, *Fath al-qadir* in Nasr et al., eds., *The Study Qur'an*, 1580.
18. Feras Hamza, Sajjad Rizvi, and Farhana Mayer, eds., *An Anthology of Qur'anic Commentaries*, Vol. 1 (London, UK. Oxford University Press, 2008), 492.

everything becomes an expression of pure will."[19] In other words, because nothing exists outside of Allah's will, because nothing happens without it being an extension of Allah, as per Al-Ghazali, then Allah *is* all things. This is why, no matter where you are or where you might turn, there you find "the Face of Allah" (S. 2:115).[20]

The inevitable implications of an unknowable deity, indistinguishable from nature and fate, ultimately result in a worldview where the distinction between Creator and creation are blurred into one. This is inevitable if God's being and knowledge is perceived as wholly different from the being and knowledge of man, for in order for there to be contact between the two, the two must fuse into one. As Van Til succinctly writes:

Either God's being and knowledge are brought down to the level of the being and knowledge of man or the being and knowledge of man are lifted up to the being and knowledge of God. There is always the same monistic assumption at work [in non-Christian world-

19. Joseph Boot, "Nature & Revelation: The Fractured Foundations of Islam," *Jubilee: Recovering Biblical Foundations for our Time*, ed. Ryan Eras, Summer 2016 (Toronto: Ezra Institute for Contemporary Christianity), 11.

20. Al-Ghazali cited in Ahad M. Ahmed, "The Theological Thought of Fazlur Rahman: A Modern Mutakkalim", *Archive*. Accessed January 9, 2017, https://archive.org/stream/thetheologicalthoughtoffazlurrahmanthesisbyahadmaqboolahmed/the-theological-thought-of-fazlur-rahman-thesis-by-ahad-maqbool-ahmed_djvu.txt/.

views] reducing all distinctions to correlatives of one another.[21]

Essentially, all worldviews that fail to provide a Creator-creation distinction fail to make sense of reality, or a more technical way of saying it would be: *All other religious worldviews fail to provide the pre-conditions for intelligibility.*

3.4 Contrary to our Being

Can man live without the biblical God then? If we mean "Can he live in rebellion and in denial of God?", then yes, of course. But that is not what we are asking here. We are asking, can he truly live, think and believe without God? The answer is no, because contrary to what the New Atheists might think, to deny the God of Christian theism is to ultimately commit intellectual suicide.

When the natural man studies his natural surroundings, he is presupposing the God of Christian theism. In fact, human beings have never stopped believing in the Christian God in their heart of hearts, for how else do we explain the reality around us? We live in such a way, for example, that expects regularity in nature. We expect language to continue to have meaning each day. We expect gravity to behave the way it does so we do not float out into outer space. We live in such a way that presupposes a personal Creator, because nature follows laws, and laws imply a lawgiver who governs creation. But why then are our thoughts and beliefs

---

21. Cornelius Van Til, *Christian Apologetics*, Second Ed. (Phillipsburg, NJ.: P&R Books, 2003), 32.

inconsistent with the way we live? Why do we deny that which we presuppose?

The Bible teaches us that we know the truth by virtue of having been created in the image of God and by the natural revelation around us. This is what Paul meant by:

> For [God's] invisible attributes, namely, his eternal power and divine nature, have been clearly perceived, ever since the creation of the world, in the things that have been made. So they are without excuse (Rom. 1:20).

When we speak of man having been created in God's image, we do not mean to say that the Creator and creation distinction has been blurred, but rather that man resembles God in every way that a creature can possibly *be* like God. That is to say, he is a personality like God, his pre-fall condition resembles God's moral attributes, he was created with "true knowledge, true righteousness, and true holiness" (Cf. Col. 3:10; Eph. 4:24).[22] What the Bible teaches is that God has self-contained being, that is to say, he is self-sufficient— while man has "created" or "derivative" being. Likewise, the Bible teaches that God has self-contained knowledge, that is to say, immediate and self-referential – while man has derivative knowledge. To put it more simply, man's being and knowledge are derived from his Creator. As Bahnsen writes in his book *Always Ready*: "God's knowledge is primary, and whatever man is to know can only be based upon a reception of what God has originally and ultimately known."[23]

---

22. Ibid., 40.
23. Greg L. Bahnsen, *Always Ready: Directions for Defending the*

But the reason for our denial of the truth is found in the very fall of man, for when Adam sought to be like God in eating the forbidden fruit, he sought to do away with God altogether, and by this I mean in every respect. He sought for his own "ideals of truth, goodness and beauty somewhere beyond God, either directly within himself or indirectly within the universe about him."[24] This was "sin", moral rebellion, the violation of God's law as laid out in the Ten Commandments, which were in the beginning placed within the very being of man (for he was created in the image of God).

Sin has ravaged the totality of man's being, it has caused a radical reversal. We have fallen from that which we were originally disposed (which was communion with God), diverted from our true nature and purpose, and ultimately led into ruin and spiritual death. This means that in the falling away from original righteousness, what takes its place as the "natural" state of man is *un*righteousness. We thus cannot help but operate in unrighteousness, and this extends to our intellectual capacities as well, what theologians refer to as the *noetic* effects of sin.

As the Bible teaches in Romans 1:18, the natural man in his sinfulness suppresses the truth, which means that the "true knowledge" which man was originally created with has not been lost, but rather, is suppressed as a form of moral rebellion. A late biblical scholar

Faith, ed. Robert R. Booth (Nacogdoches, TX.: Covenant Media Press, 2011), 19.

24. Van Til, *Christian Apologetics*, 42.

put it this way: "Everything in them and around them testifies to God, but they reject the testimony of all creation, and of their own being… to deny this revelation is for man to deny his own being."[25] It is, therefore, characteristic of the natural mind to be willfully ignorant of the God of Christian theism, even though man's antithetical worldviews are unsustainable, vain, futile, and unable to give an intelligible account of reality.

Man cannot live without God. No matter what he might try to conjure, all religious worldviews contrary to that of the Christian Scriptures can only borrow "capital" from the Christian worldview, because they cannot stand on their own presuppositions.

3.5 Christianity & Society

This, of course, has not stopped Western culture from abandoning its Christian foundation and heritage. What we have witnessed in our society of late has been an overthrow of Christian morality for a humanistic *ethos*. And the natural result of abandoning the sound truth for a baseless or foundation-less worldview is inevitable collapse and destruction. The slow and gradual deterioration that we are witnessing in our society is only a part of the Western world's incremental and systemic "death", producing nothing more than disorganization and disorder. But that is to be expected when the religious consensus of a nation is antithetical, that is to say, contrary to the very truth of inspired Scripture.

---

25. Rousas J. Rushdoony, *Romans & Galatians* (Vallecito, CA.: Ross House Books, 1997), 13.

In order that we might understand the relationship of religion and culture, and furthermore the weight of man's need for God, we must first understand what *culture* is. One Christian thinker defined "culture" this way:

> ...the public manifestation of the religious ground-motive (i.e., worship) of a people. Culture is therefore a state of being cultivated by intellectual and moral tilling in terms of a prevailing [worship] and by, natural extension, forms a particular type of civilization.[26]

As rightly expressed, this "worship" is always performed collectively in community, and is reflected in our families, education, law, art and various other spheres and institutions which shape our cultural and societal life. But what happens when you remove the true foundation of culture? As you would expect of removing the foundation from a building: inevitable collapse.

Without God's law, man has no absolute moral standard by which he can judge between right and wrong. Without God's being, man can make no distinction between the living and the non-living. Without God's knowledge, man cannot truly know what he claims to know about reality. We can speak about morality, we can speak about the nature of being, we can speak about epistemology (the acquirement of knowledge); but without God, none of these things can be known or even appropriately discussed. This will inevi-

---

26. Boot, *Gospel Culture: Living in God's Kingdom* (Toronto, ON.: Ezra Press, 2016), 3.

tably reflect in whatever culture man cultivates, whether that be a culture of religious pluralism, an Islamic culture, a Hindu culture, a postmodern culture – if it is not the true "gospel" culture, as taught and mandated by Scripture, it will collapse, and with it, human civilization. This is a part of God's judgment on the lawless man who lives in opposition to God's law-word and prefers his own man-determined morality and reality. A house built on shifting sand cannot stand.

Man needs God in order to live and think rightly, and he can only do so if he "believes" rightly. And by this, I do not mean merely believing that the God of Christian theism exists; rather, as Bahnsen had put it:

> To make God's word your presupposition, your standard, your instructor and guide… calls for renouncing intellectual self-sufficiency – the attitude that you are autonomous, able to attain unto genuine knowledge independent of God's direction and standards.[27]

This renunciation implies a change that goes far deeper than just the intellect, it constitutes a revolutionary change of our human nature, from sinful, rebellious, and corrupt to restored, sanctified, and renewed; a work that can only be carried out in the Lord Jesus Christ (Col. 3:10-12). It begins by first recognizing our spiritual, moral and epistemological brokenness and poverty; the Lordship of Christ over all things (including our own intellect); our need for a redeemer and saviour; and ultimately, putting our faith in His law-word as we walk in complete dependence

---

27. Bahnsen, *Always Ready*, 20.

on Him, which is to say, walking in faithful obedience under His sovereign grace.

When Christ, the Son of God, bore the sin of man on the cross in His flesh, He did it so that we might be restored to life and reconciled with God. As Paul had written to the Roman church: "If you confess with your mouth that Jesus is Lord and believe in your heart that God raised him from the dead, you will be saved" (Rom. 10:9), and as the apostle John had written, "If we confess our sins, he is faithful and just to forgive us our sins and to cleanse us from all unrighteousness" (1 Jn. 1:9).

It is only in Christ that we are restored to our original calling and purpose, to be God's prophet, which is to interpret our experience and reality after God (according to his law-word); to be God's priest, which is to dedicate all of creation (through culture) unto God as a form of worship; and to be God's king, which is to rule over the earth with wisdom and righteousness for, and subject to God. With this we know that the hope of Christian theism is not merely hell-fire insurance, it is the hope of realizing a godly civilization by the power of His Spirit and word, beginning with the here and now, for as Boot wisely articulated:

> [Christ] not only fulfills the *cultural role* of prophet, priest and king, just as Adam was called to do in the garden, but by his atoning death, he purchased *the right of renewal* of a new people, re-commissioned to be prophets, priests and kings in the service of God and to be his co-workers in the power of the Spirit, in the reconciling

of all things in heaven and earth to God.[28]

The world is then divided, *not* into a million pieces, reflective of all the various religious worldviews, but rather into two main people groups: the "Creator-worshippers" (that is, the *just*) and the "creation-worshippers" (that is, the *idolaters*). Which one are you? Are you engulfed by your ego-centric religion? Or have you surrendered to the truth of the gospel? What we are called to do is to repent of our sin, renounce our feigned self-sufficiency, and to take up our plows to cultivate the city of God on earth as God's faithful and redeemed representatives, upholding the truth.

Can man live without God? The ultimate and unchangeable answer is:

"No... lest he seeks to destroy himself."

---

28. Boot, *Gospel Culture*, 96.

The Problem of Evil

"Is it not from the mouth of the Most High
that good and bad come?"

– Lamentations 3:38

4.1 Introduction

WITH THREE LECTURES DOWN, we have the last, but certainly not the least, to conclude our multi-day conference. May I, at this time, briefly express how grateful I am for the warm reception you have offered me, for the opportunity to address you on your respective campuses, and the openness you have demonstrated after every lecture with your countless questions. It is with a sad heart that I depart from you, but I leave with great encouragement.

Prior to speaking on this final subject, concerning "The Problem of Evil", I would like to make clear that, from the very outset, this lecture is more than just another lecture to me. While all the lectures I have given are personal, in the sense that I firmly believe in what I teach, this lecture is perhaps far more personal given how invested my heart is in this matter. A few years ago, I lost my sister Lijia to cancer. It was a very difficult time for our family. I remember the Skype sessions we had, peering into her hospital room in Portugal. I remember the smile on her face when she received our gifts by mail, and when my father visited her in Lisbon. We mourned her loss, and for me, it was the first time that I had to deal with a death so close to home.

We may have many tragic events in mind when we speak about the problem of evil. It might even be difficult for someone who has experienced a great loss, or a great injustice, to listen to someone talk about the problem of "evil." Sometimes we think to ourselves, "What might he know about pain?" or "What might he know about injustice?" And to some degree, I can sympathize with those questions, because everyone's life experiences are different. But at the same time, not a single human being has been unaffected by the evil in our world.

4.2 The Challenge of 'Evil'

In the field of Christian apologetics, an area of my expertise, I often find that I am not dealing with a "philosophical" challenge when the problem of evil is introduced. I can recognize the unfiltered emotion, the indignation, the suffering of one who has been touched by it. There are those who try to use the problem of evil as a philosophical weapon against Christianity, but it will never be a purely intellectual challenge. It is a personal challenge, it always will be, because it has been experienced *personally*. We are all subject to the fallen conditions of our world, and as a result, sickness, tragedy, and death surrounds us, touching us either directly or indirectly. We are disturbed by its reality, and we are faced with the puzzle of why evil exists in our world, and how the biblical God could possibly allow it to exist.

The unbelieving skeptic has often hung his hat on this reality, reasoning to himself that, if there is anything that we could possibly mar the character of God with, it is the present existence of evil. In fact, going as far back as ancient Greece, we find the famous "Trilemma" of the Greek philosopher Epicurus. In the words of David Hume (1711-1776), an 18th century skeptic who simplifies Epicurus' Trilemma:

> Is [God] willing to prevent evil, but not able? Then he is impotent. Is he able, but not willing? Then he is malevolent. Is he both able and willing? Whence then is evil?[1]

We might even look at the comments of George H. Smith, who wrote in his book *Atheism: The Case Against God*:

> Briefly, the problem of evil is this... If God knows there is evil but cannot prevent it, he is not omnipotent. If God knows there is evil and can prevent it but desires not to, he is not omnibenevolent.[2]

To put it plainly, the thrust of the skeptic's argument is that either the Christian God is omnipotent or he is omni-benevolent, but by no means can he be

---

1. *Dialogues Concerning Natural Religion*, ed. Nelson Pike (Indianapolis: Bobbs-Merrill Publications, 1891), 88.

2. George H. Smith, *Atheism: The Case against God* (Buffalo, N.Y.: Prometheus Books, 1979), 81.

both. And to deny either one or the other is to deny the God of Christian theism altogether. It is no secret that Christians believe this to be true, that is, the omnipotence and omni-benevolence of God, because this is what Scripture reveals to be true. However, the skeptic believes that our set of presuppositions, or our premises, do not actually cohere or harmonize, but rather, are in conflict and contradiction with each other. I will address this philosophic challenge later on, for now, however, I want to make the counter-claim that the way the skeptic thinks and lives contradicts what he claims to believe.

The skeptic cannot treat "evil" as a purely philosophical subject. He may write on it philosophically, yes, but it is so much more than that. He has been affected by it in some way, and he has witnessed it, if not to a great degree in his own life, then in the life of others. He sincerely believes that there is such a thing as "evil", and he is both horrified and indignant about it. We might look to Richard Dawkins, a controversial but prominent atheist, who rightly referred to the murder of children at the hands of ISIS as a great "evil". He wrote: "Very few faith-heads are as *evil* as Taliban or ISIS. Yet what else but faith is capable of making people do such *evil*?"[3]

---

3. Richard Dawkins cited in Ella Alexander, "Richard Dawkins has this to say on 'evil' ISIS and Taliban after Peshawar massacre," *Independent.* Accessed October 24, 2017, http://www.independent.co.uk/news/people/richard-dawkins-has-a-strong-opinion-on-evil-isis-and-taliban-after-peshawar-massacre-9930961.html/.

We could even look at people's reactions to the news when they hear about abductions, rapes and murders. Everyone, including the staunchest of atheists, are quick to condemn such crimes as "evil". These are genuine reactions, genuine statements, and we all would agree that evil requires a response. Justice must be served. In the end, we are all, whether Christian or not, horrified and indignant about the evil acts committed in our world.

I remember a few years ago listening to a lecture by the apologist Greg L. Bahnsen on the problem of evil. He had mentioned that on a radio show, where he was being interviewed, someone called in to challenge his belief in God. He wrote of his experience in his book *Always Ready*, saying:

> The caller wanted to know how anybody could adore a God who permitted sexual abuse and mutilation of a baby, such as the caller had witnessed in certain courtroom photographs at the trial of some horrible specimen of humanity… I knew the caller meant to press his hostility to Christianity upon me hard, but I was actually glad that the caller was so irate. He was taking evil *seriously*. His condemnation of child abuse was not simply a matter of personal preference to him.[4]

Let me repeat that last part to you, "he was taking evil *seriously*." Do you know why this is important? Because it means that the caller was using some stan-

---

4.   Greg L. Bahnsen, *Always Ready: Directions for Defending the Faith*, ed. Robert R. Booth (Nacogdoches, TX.: Covenant Media Press, 2011), 165.

dard by which to determine what is good and evil. He does not regard evil as something purely philosophical, or "preferential", but rather as something "objective" and "absolute" which cannot be called good. Dawkins does this by condemning the actions of ISIS, people do this by condemning evil acts in our society, *you* do this when you recognize that you have been wronged in some way. The skeptic might want to believe that the reality of evil is a solid philosophical challenge against Christian theism, but by referencing the reality of evil, instead of highlighting a contradiction within the Christian religious worldview, he has instead revealed his own contradiction, that what he refers to as "evil" can only be rightfully called "evil" from within the Christian worldview.

The same can be said for the skeptic who claims that a loving God cannot exist while genocides, infanticides, and famines take place. As a Christian, I cannot make light of these things. Scripture teaches these things to be evil, for in the acts against man, these are violations of God's sovereign law and a great offence against those created equally in God's image, and for the events of nature, it is apparent to us that this world is not what it ought to be (or for that matter, what it once was prior to the fall of man). We call this what it is, ugly, horrendous, tragic and unfortunately, real. The evil in our world is not illusory as the Hindu or the Buddhist would like you to believe. The Hindu claims that evil is nothing more than the playful manifestation of *Brahman*, the impersonal god of all things, and therefore bearing no distinction from that which is good. The Buddhist claims that evil is an illusion and a distraction from the true objective of man, to be one with Nirvana, the vast nothingness of all things. Whether it be the skeptic, the Hindu, the Buddhist, or any other person who rejects the truth of Christian theism, these questions need to be asked: How can someone make sense of their indignation? How can someone condemn an action or tragic event as "evil"? How can one justify their moral judgment from their own atheistic, Hindu, or Buddhist worldview with their respective presuppositions?

Let me unpack that for you.

4.3 The Unbeliever's Absent Foundation

In order for the skeptic to challenge Christian theism with the existence of evil, he must first be able to assert that there is in fact "evil" in this world. He might point to the evil around us, to the injustice, to the suffering, to death, etc. I would most readily grant that there is in fact evil in this world, and that this is evident to all human beings. But how does the skeptic *conclude* that such a thing is evil?

Here is one of the responses I have received: "Whatever is good is whatever evokes public approval, and whatever is evil is whatever evokes public disapproval." Let me illustrate for you the futility, or absurdity, of such thinking.

In the case of Nazi Germany, culminating in World War II, Hitler's regime had changed national law in order to "legally" persecute Jews and other minorities. The holocaust was therefore "legal" within the political and social context of Nazi Germany, and this was the result of wide-spread public approval which allowed Hitler to become the third Reich. If this is in fact the standard by which we can distinguish between good and evil, then the holocaust could not be deemed as "evil." Bahnsen put it this way: To say that "the vast majority of the community heartily approved of and willingly joined in the evil deed" could never make sense.[5]

However, the skeptic might nonetheless say: "That is not true though. The holocaust was evil, it has been considered a severe war crime." Why does the skeptic say this? Because unbeknownst to him, the property of an action, thing, or personal trait as either good or evil is irrelevant to what one might feel, think or believe. He cannot help but be this way because he has been *wired* this way, he is a moral agent created in the *imago Dei* (image of God) with the consciousness of the law of God within him. To deny this biblical truth, and to be consistent with skepticism or naturalism, is to subject oneself to irrational subjectivism, where then no objective ethical judgments can be made and where society would inevitably collapse, paving the way to nihilism (the meaninglessness of all things).

But then the other response I get from skeptics is that: "An action or trait is good if it tends to achieve a certain end, like the greatest happiness of the greatest number, and whatever is opposite of that is evil." But how might one determine that? Would this not involve

---

5.   Ibid., 168.

rating and comparing happiness, and then calculating all of the consequences of any given action or trait? The infinite factors involved would make this mathematically impossible for the finite mind. And any theory that asserts the goodness or evil of a certain consequence must first establish that such a consequence is good or evil.

Philosophically, the existence of evil actually proves to be a problem for the unbeliever. He rightly identifies certain things in our world as evil, whether that be child molestation, genocide, murder, disease, etc. But he cannot, from his own worldview (or perspective of reality) make sense of *why* such things are evil. In other words, he cannot legitimately explain his underlying philosophy of evil in such a way that justifies his moral indignation. Why is that? Because by eliminating the God of Christian theism from the moral equation, atheism (or secular humanism) introduces in its place a "survival of the fittest" philosophy of life, where life, death, and suffering are essentially meaningless. If the unbeliever were to be consistent with his own worldview, then he would never be able to take evil *seriously*, instead, he would have to be indifferent to it.

In a debate that I had almost six years ago at York University, I was challenged by two atheists on the existence of God. In one of their rebuttals, they claimed that God could not exist in a world filled with evil. I responded by asking them how they knew what was good and evil. They could rightly identify evil, but they could not explain why something *is* evil. And when I asked what standard they were using to differentiate between good and evil, they could not help but say "We do not really know."

The truth is, there is no moral foundation for skepticism, naturalism or atheism. As a matter of fact, any non-Christian worldview is morally baseless, that is, missing its foundation, and as a result, it cannot help but *borrow* capital from the Christian worldview. How so? By asserting that there is such a thing as evil, we are asserting that there is such a thing as good. And by asserting that there is such a thing as good *and* evil, we are implying a moral standard by which we can differentiate between the two. And by implying a moral standard we imply a moral lawgiver, and given that man cannot be that lawgiver, we are essentially presupposing the God of Christian theism who unbelievers are attempting to disprove. Cornelius Van Til captures this image perfectly, a quote so good that I cannot help but cite it again after our previous lecture: "A little child may slap his father in the face, but he can do so only because the father holds him on his knee."[6]

4.4 Philosophical or Psychological?

So while the unbeliever has no good, legitimate reason to consider anything "evil", despite their appeal to personal choice or feeling (which I have shown to be insufficient), the Christian can make perfect sense of his own revulsion because his standard is found in the "absolute, unchanging and good character of God."[7]

---

6. Cornelius Van Til, *The Case for Calvinism* (Phillipsburg, NJ.: P&R Publishing, 1979), 147-148.

7. Bahnsen, *Always Ready*, 170.

As Bahnsen writes, "The expression of moral indignation is but personal evidence that unbelievers know this God in their heart of hearts."[8]

This is what the Christian, the skeptic, the atheist, the naturalist, the Hindu, the Buddhist, and all others hold in common. We know the truth by virtue of being created in God's image, and by being surrounded by his natural revelation in creation. The difference, however, is that the non-Christian suppresses this truth by his rebellion against God's sovereignty. He seeks autonomy, to be independent from God existentially, epistemologically, and morally. And so, he cannot help but craft his own worldview while turning a blind eye to the fact that he must borrow from the Christian worldview (the right perception of reality) in order to think and live in God's world. The Christian once thought and lived this way, until he had been rescued from his own futility, forgiven of his sins by God's grace, and transformed in the core of his being by the Spirit of God. He now sees clearly through the lens of Scripture, which corrects his fallible perception.

I hope that, up to this point, I have been able to illustrate to you the inconsistency and contradiction of the unbeliever as it relates to the reality of evil. Let me now respond to the argument that is often levied against Christian theism, the skeptic's challenge:

1. God is All-Good;
2. God is All-Powerful;
3. Evil Exists

---

8. Ibid.

The contradiction should be apparent. Or is it? The argument is that, based on these three premises, God cannot be both all-good and all-powerful, because evil exists. But this argument is framed by the skeptic's worldview, his perception of reality, and as a result, his definition of "good" and "powerful" and "evil" are different than the Christian's. In order for me to respond to this argument, I need to adopt the very same presuppositions of Scripture (what it teaches to be true), and not that of the skeptic.

Does the Bible teach that God is all-good? Yes, it reveals this in the following passages:

> **1 Chronicles 16:34** - "O give thanks to the LORD, for He is good; For His lovingkindness is everlasting."

> **Psalm 119:68** - "You [God] are good and do good; Teach me Your statutes."

> **Psalm 145:9** - "The LORD is good to all, And His mercies are over all His works."

> **Nahum 1:7** - "The LORD is good, A stronghold in the day of trouble, And He knows those who take refuge in Him."

> **Matthew 19:17** - "And Jesus said to him, 'Why are you asking Me about what is good? There is only One [God] who is good; but if you wish to enter into life, keep the commandments."

Does the Bible also teach that God is all-powerful? Yes, it reveals this too in the following passages:

Isaiah 43:13 - "Even from eternity I am He, And there is none who can deliver out of My hand; I act and who can reverse it?'"

Jeremiah 32:27 - "Behold, I am the LORD, the God of all flesh; is anything too difficult for Me?"

Daniel 4:35 - "All the inhabitants of the earth are accounted as nothing, But He does according to His will in the host of heaven And among the inhabitants of earth; And no one can ward off His hand Or say to Him, 'What have you done?'"

Matthew 19:26 - "And looking at them Jesus said to them, 'With people this is impossible, but with God all things are possible.'"

Now, if I am to be consistent with my biblical presuppositions, I can only see "evil" in light of God's all-goodness. In other words, I have to infer that God has a "morally good reason for the evil that exists," for he cannot be overwhelmed by evil given his omnipotence. As Bahnsen puts it, "God has planned evil events for reasons which are morally commendable and good."[9] That might seem difficult to swallow, and I will address that reality shortly. But the solution to the three premises that is often presented by the skeptic is the addition of a fourth premise:

4. God has a Morally Sufficient Reason for the Evil which Exists

---

9. Ibid., 172.

What might be a biblical example of this? Well, we can consider the crucifixion of Jesus. Ask yourself the question, "Was it evil that Jesus was killed?" He lived a morally perfect life, performed signs and wonders to restore that which was broken, sick, and dead. He was the holiest of all men because He is the Holy of Holies, the Second Person of the Triune Godhead, eternally begotten of the Father, and of the same substance as God. His teachings exposed the false teachings of the religious authorities of his day, and out of jealousy for both his influence and authority, he was killed. Was the killing of Christ therefore evil? Yes, it was a great evil in fact. An innocent man (innocent before God on all accounts) was given a criminal's death. The bodily manifestation of God was abused by fallen, sinful man. But God had a *morally sufficient* reason for that evil, it was for the redemption, salvation and renewal of man and creation. That by the death of Christ, he might serve as a substitution for the payment of our penalty (of sin), our violations of God's law, for all those who believe.

This serves as a supreme example in Scripture as to why God would allow evil to run its course, because in the end, God uses evil for a supreme purpose. Consider what I say, God "uses" evil to serve His will and purpose, He is NOT the cause or origin of evil.

Abraham, whom was credited as being the friend of God, was asked to sacrifice his son Isaac, and what was it that Abraham said? Genesis 18:25 says "Shall not the Judge of all the earth do what is *just*?" This story, in particular, seems disturbing. But did God allow

Abraham to sacrifice his son? No, he did not. Instead, He stopped him and provided Abraham with a ram for the sacrifice of atonement. The sacrifice of atonement was a prophetic symbol of the sacrifice on the cross in the New Testament, and the image of a father sacrificing his own son was also a prophetic symbol of what God would do for mankind, providing for the penalty of our sin as He provided the ram for Abraham.

The problem, as you can see, is that the reality of evil is not philosophical. No, it is psychological. Because the truth is, we might be able to see the coherence of the Christian worldview, how it corresponds to reality, how we can make sense of reality from the lens of Scripture, but we emotionally struggle to accept the reality of evil.

The biblical book of Job, for example, presents us with a godly man who is blessed with a large family, good health, and financial prosperity, but he suddenly loses everything. Throughout the book, God does not provide an explanation to Job as to why he is allowed to suffer such things. As it concerns the direct answer, Job is not given one. He is, however, given a vast tour of the many created wonders of God, by God Himself, and he explores the great complexity of God's creation under His divine sovereignty. Job arrives at the realization that finite man cannot fully comprehend the ways of the infinite God, for what we see in part, God sees in full.

As we walk in our fallen world, we need to come to grips with the fact that God rarely gives us a full explanation as to why something evil might occur, and the truth is, He has no obligation to do so. We as creatures bearing the image of God are His creation, and He is the Creator. And as Deuteronomy 29:29 states: "The secret things belong to the LORD our God." You might object and say, "This cannot be! The intelligibility of the Christian faith rests upon the knowability of God," but what we know of God through His revelation, both in Scripture and creation, is sufficient. We need to bear in mind that, as creatures, we can never think on the same level as the Creator, and so there are things that the Creator might do or say that we as creatures may not fully understand. As God stated through His prophet Isaiah: "For as the heavens are higher than the earth, so are my ways higher than your ways and my thoughts than your thoughts" (Isa. 55:9).

What God has revealed about Himself, however, makes clear that God is not the cause or author of misery, suffering and injustice – as He has defined these in His word. They are, however, a part of God's overarching plan for history and for our individual lives. For the Christian (like myself), this is emotionally difficult to comprehend, but Christians do not walk by "sight" as the materialists do, we walk by *faith*, trusting in God's written and creational revelation. For the unbelieving skeptic, this is often too intolerable for his own pride and self-centered reason, because, after all, faithful to the spirit of pretended autonomy (or independence from God) which our first parents sought, man would rather *serve as a judge over God* than to be subject to and judged by God.

4.5 The Response to Evil

We have thus far been able to see (i) the inconsistency of the unbeliever's presuppositions as it concerns the existence of evil, and distinguish evil as (ii) a psychological and not a philosophical problem for Christian theism. Let me now conclude by telling you what the Christian response to the reality of evil is, beginning first with its entry into our created world:

The creation narrative recorded in Genesis tells us that when Adam and Eve were created, they were morally and spiritually good. They reflected the very righteousness of their Creator because they bore his image, and as a result, their knowledge of good and evil was derived from their primary knowledge of God. It was a derived knowledge, not a personally experienced knowledge.[10] But when they were tempted by the serpent, the act of disobedience and rebellion that they had committed against God was not, at root, in the eating of the forbidden fruit (though this was a violation of God's command), but in the motive behind the act, which was to seek existential, epistemological and moral independence from God. In other words, to be like God, their Creator, in a way that was unbefitting for a created creature. By separating himself from God, and this meant discarding His authoritative law-word and just government, man brought forth the curse of sin which has ravaged the world with sickness, death and

---

10. Though they experienced God's goodness, they had not experienced evil, in any case, their primary source of knowledge was the knowledge of God, they did not look for another *primary* source until the moment of the fall.

corruption. It has spread like a genetic disease to all members of the human race, and whether we would like to admit it or not, it has marred our human nature.

As C.S. Lewis, author of *The Chronicles of Narnia*, depicted in his Narnian cosmology, the son of Adam had opened the door for evil to ran rampant in the created world:

> "You see, friends," he [Aslan] said, "that before the new, clean world I gave you is seven hours old, a force of evil has already entered it; waked and brought hither by this son of Adam... Evil will come of that evil... And as Adam's race has done the harm, Adam's race shall help to heal it."[11]

Could God have prevented this evil from occurring? By all means, of course. Was it His will to prevent this from happening? Though God does not desire that anyone should disobey Him, He willed that man might commit the mistake by his own volition. But we must bear in mind the presuppositions of Scripture, God has a *morally sufficient* reason for allowing this evil to occur.

Perhaps one day we might be granted the privilege to look back from eternity into the past and discern the wondrous and glorious work of God in the midst of, and through the evil that we have witnessed. But whether we will be granted this privilege or not, Scripture makes clear that God does not find pleasure in evil. He hates it, and it will be destroyed at the appoint-

---

11. C.S. Lewis, *The Magician's Nephew* (New York, NY.: Harper-Collins Publishers, 2002), 162.

ed time that He has set. God shall execute absolute and righteous judgment, and nothing done under the sun shall escape His eyes.

To even consider that God is idle while evil persists is erroneous; He does not sit with crossed arms somewhere outside of creation while the earth burns away in fire. He has, in fact, done something about it, He sent His Son in human flesh to be the atonement for our sins, that in his life, death and resurrection we might find redemption, renewal and restoration. God offers to restore man to his true nature, where his goodness might be found, not in his corrupted self, but in the perfect man of God, Jesus Christ.

To this day, God continues to produce a transformation within the hearts of men, one which restores their ways to righteousness, undoing the effects of the fall. He has also promised us a world without pain and suffering, along with the renewal of all things, that those who repent and surrender to His reign might enjoy this new creation as their inheritance. All this He is accomplishing and will bring to completion in His appointed time as His kingdom (just government) is made fully manifest in history. As Paul stated to the Corinthians, "For he [Christ] must reign until he has put all his enemies under his feet. The last enemy to be destroyed is death" (1 Cor. 15:25-26).

I had cited the philosopher and writer C.S. Lewis for a reason, he was a man who was profoundly impacted by the evil of our world. He fought against it personally, witnessed horrid deaths, and suffered from it in such great depths, but instead of it keeping him away from God, he was drawn to the truth of Christian theism. His early atheism had nothing meaningful to say to the evil around him, because in the end he knew it to be a lie, a very comfortable lie. As Lewis subtly said, to be removed from this comfortable lie involved much kicking and screaming,[12] but in his newfound faith in Christ he remained steadfast, even after the loss of his wife.[13]

You see, both Lewis and J.R.R. Tolkien fought in the Great War, they were your standard foot soldiers, and as Joseph Loconte writes in his book *A Hobbit, a Wardrobe, and a Great War*, it was:

> ...nevertheless, belief in the existence of a moral order to the universe [that] helped these authors [Tolkien and Lewis] to confront the human predicament: the diabolical and deeply rooted challenges to justice and peace in our world.[14]

Tolkien, the close friend of Lewis, depicted the gross reality of evil in his literary work *The Lord of the Rings*. As Loconte illustrates:

> On the desolate path to Mordor we encounter "dead grasses and rotting reeds" that "loomed up in the mists like ragged shadows of long-forgotten summers." We

---

12. C.S. Lewis, *Surprised by Joy: The Shape of My Early Life* (San Francisco, CA.: HarperOne, 2017), 279.

13. See C.S. Lewis, *A Grief Observed* (San Francisco, CA.: HarperOne, 2009).

14. Joseph Loconte, *A Hobbit, a Wardrobe, and a Great War: How J.R.R. Tolkien and C.S. Lewis Rediscovered Faith, Friendship, and Heroism in the Great War* (Nashville, TN.: Thomas Nelson, 2015), Kindle Edition, 52.

see "a land defiled, diseased beyond healing." We watch Sam Gamgee, during the passage through the marshes, catch his foot and fall on his hands, "which sank deep into sticky ooze, so that his face was brought close to the surface of the dark mire." Looking intently into the glazed and grimy muck, he is startled by what he finally sees. "There are dead things, dead faces in the water," he said with horror. "Dead faces!" Gollum laughed. "The Dead Marshes, yes, yes: that is their name," he crackled.[15]

This was Tolkien's experience in the battle of Sommes, the horrid experience of discovering rotting corpses undisturbed except by the blasts of artillery. It was heart-wrenching, it was gruesome, and it would only be a glimpse of what the next World War would bring. I cannot fathom how difficult these experiences were for Lewis and Tolkien, but I can admire and imitate both their faith and trust in God in spite of all the evil they witnessed. As Tolkien subtlety conveyed in his fictional narrative: "Even when I was far away,' says Gandalf, 'there has never been a day when the Shire has not been guarded by watchful eyes.'"[16]

Yes, God remained in control. He is still sovereign, always will be, and there is a morally sufficient reason for the evil that exists. We are, in the meantime, to trust Him, to have faith *in* Him, to know that one day we will look back and understand. This is why Christians, as God's vice-regents, are to shine brightly in the

15. Ibid., 73.
16. Cited in ibid., 50.

midst of evil. Not only in our confession of the gospel of grace, but in the embodiment of the hope of the saints, participating in God's grand redemption story. To re-iterate the words from *The Magician's Nephew*: "...as Adam's race has done the harm, Adam's race shall help to heal it."[17]

This may be in acts of compassion, weeping with those who weep, helping those in need, and fighting for the helpless and defenseless. The Canadian Coalition for Bio-Ethical Reform, for example, fights for the rights of the unborn, protesting against the mass murder of babies. The Association of Reformed Political Action has been doing their part in trying to change public and political opinion on doctor-assisted suicide to protect the elderly and the sick. Compassion Canada sponsors children in third world countries for the provision of their basic needs. These are but a few of several Christian organizations working towards combating our world's evils, and these are all considered worthy, Christ-centered kingdom work, that is to say, work involving the advancement of God's just governance by the application of His word to every area of life. But it all begins by recognizing who we are in the face of a holy God, recognizing our own sin, our need for salvation and renewal, and our call as beings created in the image of God to be subject to, and to advance God's kingdom, so that by the restorative power of God, evil might be destroyed. For the gospel first brings forth renewal in our hearts, and from there it flows out to every area of our lives, and will one day

---

17. C.S. Lewis, *The Magician's Nephew*, 162.

encompass the whole world with the culmination of Christ's second advent, who will return as the perfect and righteous judge. And what joy that day will bring.

I cite, in closing, the passage which sums up the Christian hope (and my hope) for the restoration of all things, Revelation 21:1-8. A passage that Lewis and Tolkien alluded to in the conclusions of their fictional narratives. A passage which resonates with the universal human desire to return to Eden, and for justice to be administered once and for all:

> Then I saw a new heaven and a new earth, for the first heaven and the first earth had passed away, and the sea was no more. And I saw the holy city, new Jerusalem, coming down out of heaven from God, prepared as a bride adorned for her husband. And I heard a loud voice from the throne saying, 'Behold, the dwelling place of God is with man. He will dwell with them, and they will be his people, and God himself will be with them as their God. He will wipe every tear from their eyes, and death shall be no more, neither shall there be mourning, nor crying, nor pain anymore, for the former things have passed away.' And he who was seated on the throne said, 'Behold, I am making all things new.' Also he said, 'Write this down, for these words are trustworthy and true.' And he said to me, 'It is done! I am the Alpha and the Omega, the beginning and the end. To the thirsty I will give from the spring of the water of life without payment. The one who conquers will have this heritage, and I will be his God and he will be my son. But as for the cowardly, the faithless, the detestable, as for murderers, the sexually immoral,

sorcerers, idolaters, and all liars, their portion will be in the lake that burns with fire and sulfur, which is the second death.

APPENDIX I:
The Muslim & Christian Mind

5.1 Epistemic Foundations

WE ALL CLAIM TO KNOW THINGS. At times, we agree on what we know about reality, at other times, we disagree. But if there is something that is undeniable to both the unbeliever and the Christian, it is that we all have knowledge of something. Consider, for example, the Muslim and the Christian. Both will agree that they know that each other exists, they are not thinking of a non-existent religious group when they refer to one another. They also know that they themselves exist, for otherwise they could not think, speak or be. But just as they agree on certain "facts" about reality, they also disagree with each other about the underlying *philosophy* of those facts. The Muslim claims that Islam is the only rational worldview from which we can understand the facts of reality, while the Christian makes the same claim about the Christian religious worldview. A "worldview" can be defined as:

> A network of presuppositions (which are not verified by the procedures of natural science) regarding reality (metaphysics), knowing (epistemology), and conduct (ethics) in terms of which every element of human experience is related and interpreted.[1]

The question ultimately is, How do we know that we know such a thing? And do we *truly* know reality, that is, can we make sense of what we know? Every person has their own presuppositions, beliefs which they presuppose to be true, but how can we validate these presuppositions? What we are essentially asking is whether the Islamic or the Christian worldview provides the pre-conditions of intelligibility, and in order to answer this, the epistemic foundations of each worldview need to be considered.

Epistemology, derived from the Greek *episteme*, is defined as "the theory of knowledge, especially with regard to its methods, validity and scope, and the distinction between justified belief and opinion."[2] The epistemic foundation is essentially determined by what a person presupposes to be true about reality, what they believe about God and man, Creator and creation. The purpose of this paper is to demonstrate how the Islamic worldview fails in providing the preconditions

---

1. Gary DeMar, ed., *Pushing the Antithesis: The Apologetic Methodology of Greg L. Bahnsen* (Powder Springs, GA.: American Vision Press, 2010), 42-43.

2. Oxford University Press, "Epistemology," *English Oxford Living Dictionaries.* Accessed January 10, 2017, https://en.oxforddictionaries.com/definition/epistemology.

of intelligibility from two fronts relating to the predication of reality. These are (i) the doctrine of Allah, and (ii) the doctrine of man. If the Muslim cannot make sense of that which he knows, if he cannot *truly* know reality, then it matters not what he might say about the Qur'an, Isa (the Qur'anic Jesus), Muhammad, or sharia law; everything within the Islamic system of thought would be reduced to futility. In contrast to this, this paper will also demonstrate how the Christian worldview succeeds in providing the pre-conditions of intelligibility, particularly where Islam fails. This means that the Christian can *truly* know reality, he can make sense of what he knows, because his presuppositions are both true and valid.

5.2 The Starting Point

In order to analyze the epistemic foundation of the Islamic worldview, we first need to understand the "knowledge transaction of man," such as identifying where his starting point is, and whether that starting point in his thinking is an 'immediate' or an 'ultimate' starting point.[3] As the example cited above, the Muslim and the Christian are able to acknowledge the "fact" that each other exists, this would be considered their immediate starting point of everyday experience, but not necessarily their ultimate starting point, at least not for the Christian. The Christian philosopher Cornelius Van Til helps to clarify this in his analogy of the diver. In his *A Survey of Christian Epistemology*, he presents the

---

3. Cornelius Van Til, *A Survey of Christian Epistemology, Vol. 2 of the Series In Defense of Biblical Christianity* (Phillipsburg, NJ.: Presbyterian and Reformed Publishing Co., 1969), 106.

illustration of a diver standing at the tip of a diving board, and all that he can see is the tip on which he is standing and the water all around him. If he were to refer to the tip of the diving board as his starting point, he could mean either of two things: If he were ignorant of the connection between the diving board and its concrete base, he would mean that the tip is his permanent or ultimate starting point. If he were aware of the connection between the diving board and its concrete base, he would mean that the tip is his immediate starting point.[4]

The task before us then is to discern the ultimate starting point for the Muslim mind, which, though it is often stated to be the revelation of the Qur'an, is actually man's own finite consciousness. This is evident in the dialectical tension within the Qur'anic text, depicting knowledge as solely that of Allah (S. 49:16), while also regarding man as the ultimate reference point (S. 45:3-4); the natural result of a counterfeit religion which has borrowed from the Christian worldview, while at the same time preserving man's desire for epistemological, moral and existential autonomy.

5.3 The First Front: The Doctrine of Allah

In order to accurately portray Islamic theology, the doctrine of Allah must be primarily derived from the teachings of the Qur'an, but we can also consult published commentaries from Muslim scholars who aid us in understanding Islamic thought and its history of interpretation. For example, the Qur'an opens its first

---

4. Ibid.

surah by describing Allah as the "Compassionate," the "Merciful," the "Lord of the worlds" and the "Master of the Day of Judgment" (S. 1:1-4). The reason for this opening of praise is given by the 10th century commentator al-Qushayri, who states that because of Allah's elevated status as deity, "God has praised Himself in this opening address so that human beings can praise God in the speech of God, since God knows that they cannot praise Him fully in their own words."[5] This is because nothing in creation "resembles [Allah] in any respect," he is unique, one, and "The One." As Islamic theologians of past and present have asserted, Allah in his oneness is self-sustained, the "Willer of existing things" and all things that will come to exist.[6]

Al-Asharia (AD 874-936) and al-Ghazali (AD 1058-1111), Islamic commentators, provide us with six attributes of Allah which have been prevalent in Islamic thought: (i) life; (ii) knowledge; (iii) hearing; (iv) sight; (v) will and (vi) speech; which, as scholar George Foot Moore writes, "are inherent in the divine essence, eternal, and unchangeable."[7] These attributes, however, are rooted in the cornerstone of the Islamic worldview, the fundamental doctrine which all other doctrines are

5.   Abu'l-Qasim al-Qushayri, *Lata'if al-isharat* cited in *Seyyed Hossein Nasr* et al., eds., *The Study Qur'an: A New Translation and Commentary* (New York, N.Y.: Harper Collins Publishers, 2015), 6.

6.   Rick Richter, ed., *Comparing the Qur'an and the Bible* (Grand Rapids, MI.: BakerBooks, 2011), 41.

7.   George Foot Moore, *History of Religions, Vol. 2: Judaism, Christianity, Mohammedanism* (New York, NY.: Charles Scribner's Sons, 1919), 475.

built on:[8] the Qur'anic teaching of the 'absolute unity' of Allah (*tawhid*).[9] It is the unity and singularity of Allah's oneness that makes Islam, in the Muslim's mind, the "purest form of monotheism."[10] This oneness of Allah is inseparable from the doctrine of *tanzih*, which as the modern scholar M. Azram describes: "everything [creation] is separate and different from Him [Allah] as a Creator."[11] This is derived from the surah of *al-Ikhlas* where Allah is depicted as "absolutely transcendent," not bearing any likeness with creation, and yet, as per Qur'anic literature, immanent in all creation, for "wheresoever you turn, there is the Face of God" (S. 2:115).[12]

How then can we understand the relationship between Allah and his creation? Mirza Tahir Ahmad cites Einstein's tribute to the "symmetry in nature" in his *An Elementary Study of Islam*, stating that absolute harmony in Allah's creations requires the "oneness of creator."[13] In fact, he goes on to say that the doctrine of *tawhid* is

---

8.   Mirza Tahir Ahmad, *An Elementary Study of Islam* (Tilford, Surrey: Islam International Publications Ltd., 2010), 7.

9.   Normal L. Geisler and Abdul Saleeb, *Answering Islam: The Crescent in Light of the Cross*, Updated & Revised ed. (Grand Rapids, MI.: BakerBooks, 2002), 19-20.

10. Alhaj A. D. Ajijola, *The Essence of Faith in Islam* (Lahore, Pakistan: Islamic Publications Ltd., 1978), 55.

11. M. Azram, "Epistemology: An Islamic Perspective," *IIUM Engineering Journal* 12, no. 5 (2011), 183.

12. The commentaries of Shihab al-Din al-Alusi, *Ruh al-ma ani fi tafsir al-Qur'an al-azim wa'l-sab al-mathani* and Muhammad ibn Ali al-Shawkani, *Fath al-qadir* in Nasr et al., eds., *The Study Qur'an*, 1580.

13. T. Ahmad, *An Elementary Study of Islam*, 9.

essential for human education and civilization because it brings unity (he also uses the term 'consistency') to "man's views and actions."[14] T. Ahmad makes an argument from necessity, that the doctrine of Allah is true because it serves the good of man; and thus, it is reasoned, that by presupposing the singularity of Allah, predication of reality is made possible, that is to say, we can attribute meaning to and make sense of reality. But the implications of the Islamic doctrine of God renders this assertion absolutely false.

According to modern day scholarship, the doctrine of *tawhid* is the "central point of Islamic epistemology."[15] To be successful in the acquirement of true knowledge, there are three stages of self-consciousness relating to *tawhid* that man must first fulfill. The first is to believe in the oneness of Allah and to feel "the essence of *tawhid* as an illumination inside one's mind."[16] The second is to confess the monotheism of Allah and his prophet, and the third is to apply this confession to daily life.[17] However, given the doctrine of *tanzih*, the complete 'otherness' and pure transcendence of Allah, to say anything about Allah theologically, or to even think and conceptualize Allah, is to render him "knowable", which according to

14. Ibid., 10.
15. Md. Abdus Salam and Sanober S. Shaikh, "Is there an Islamic epistemology? Role of HRD," National Institute of Development Administration: Bangkok, Thailand, 2014. Accessed January 9, 2017, http://www.ufhrd.co.uk/wordpress/wp-content/uploads/2014/11/Abdus-Salam1.pdf/.
16. Ibid.
17. Ibid.

Islam is *shirk*, the erroneous association of him with anything else. As the commentator Fadl Allah writes, "The mental faculty cannot reach Him in His elusive and hidden mystery."[18] Allah is essentially unknowable, inapproachable, unintelligible, because there ultimately exists no possible likeness between him and creation. T. Ahmad's claim, therefore, of the harmony and unity of the created universe requiring the oneness of a creator is essentially *shirk*. For to say anything about Allah results in him ceasing to be an absolute and incomparable unity. No theology is therefore possible, no knowledge of the divine is intelligible, because Allah is beyond human understanding. As the Christian philosopher Joe Boot writes: "This abstraction of Allah as *tawhid* is not unlike the Greek idea of an absolute unity or oneness found in the thought of Plotinus."[19] For to say anything about such a singular being would be impossible, considering that nothing can be said about the unknowable (S. 42:51).

But as we delve further into the doctrine of Allah, we find that not only is Allah depicted as an unknowable, isolated singularity, he is also by implication 'pantheistic.' Despite all claims to the contrary of Islam's pure monotheism, the Qur'an describes Allah as the Willer of all things, and as a result becomes "in-

---

18. Feras Hamza, Sajjad Rizvi, and Farhana Mayer, eds., *An Anthology of Qur'anic Commentaries*, Vol. 1 (London, UK.: Oxford University Press, 2008), 492.

19. Joseph Boot, "Nature & Revelation: The Fractured Foundations of Islam," *Jubilee: Recovering Biblical Foundations for our Time*, ed. Ryan Eras, Summer 2016 (Toronto: Ezra Institute for Contemporary Christianity), 11.

distinguishable from 'nature' and 'fate' itself, because everything becomes an expression of pure will."[20] In other words, because nothing exists outside of Allah's will, because nothing happens without it being an extension of Allah, as per Al-Ghazali, then Allah *is* all things. This is why, no matter where you are or where you might turn, there you find "the Face of Allah" (S. 2:115).[21] As Al-Ghazali writes:

> Indeed there is nothing in existence except God and His acts, for whatever is there besides Him is His act…. [mystics] are able to see visually that there is no being in the world other than God and that the face of everything is perishable save His face (S. 28:88) … indeed, everything other than He, considered in itself, is pure non-being …therefore, nothing is except God Almighty and His face.[22]

The implications of an unknowable deity, indistinguishable from nature and fate, ultimately result in a 'Oneist' worldview, where all distinctions between Creator and creation are blurred into one. This is inevitable if God's being and knowledge is perceived as wholly different from the being and knowledge of man, for

---

20. Ibid., 12.
21. Al-Ghazali cited in Ahad M. Ahmed, "The Theological Thought of Fazlur Rahman: A Modern Mutakkalim," *Archive*. Accessed January 9, 2017, https://archive.org/stream/thetheologicalthoughtoffazlurrahmanthesisbyahadmaqboolahmed/the-theological-thought-of-fazlur-rahman-thesis-by-ahad-maqbool-ahmed_djvu.txt/.
22. Al-Ghazali, cited in Robert R. Reilly, *The Closing of the Muslim Mind: How Intellectual Suicide Created the Modern Islamist Crisis* (Wilmington, DE.: ISI Books, 2010), 110.

in order for there to be contact between the two, the two must fuse into one. As Van Til writes:

> Either God's being and knowledge are brought down to the level of the being and knowledge of man or the being and knowledge of man are lifted up to the being and knowledge of God. There is always the same monistic assumption at work reducing all distinctions to correlatives of one another.[23]

For what can be said of Allah? Nothing. We know nothing about the true nature of Allah, nor what distinguishes him from creation. We are left to assume, as per the Qur'anic text, that Allah, fate, and nature are one and the same.

Ironically, T. Ahmad admits to this 'Oneist' implication, stating that the principle of God's oneness "does not permit people to create divisions between God and His creation and within the creation of God."[24] This means that we cannot make a distinction between good and evil, male and female, or even between the numbers 1, 2, 3, etc. if all is Allah and Allah is all, for there cannot be any distinctions in an unknowable, pure oneness. Essentially, both the doctrines of *tawhid* and *tanzih*, which are fundamental to the doctrine of Allah, result in a breakdown of knowledge, failing to justify the intelligibility of reality, and instead implying the opposite, that reality should be unintelligible, meaningless extensions of the all-pervading oneness of Allah.

---

23. Van Til, *Christian Apologetics*, Second ed. (NJ.: Presbyterian & Reformed Publishing, 2003), 32.

24 T. Ahmad, *An Elementary Study of Islam*, 10.

5.4 The Second Front: The Doctrine of Man

The doctrine of Allah, however, is not isolated from the other doctrines of Islamic theology, for it functions as part of a systematic whole. We cannot sever it from the Islamic doctrine of man, for example, which suffers as a result of the implications of Allah's pure oneness and transcendence. But on its own, the doctrine of man also poses serious problems for Islam's attempt to predicate (make sense of) reality.

When consulting the Qur'anic text, we read that mankind was created from "potter's clay of black mud altered" (S. 15:26), brought from death to life by the power of Allah. However, contrary to the Christian notion of man being created in the "image of God", Qur'anic literature refers to man as just another creature, but also as Allah's caliph on earth, his vice-regency (S. 2:30), in which man is tasked with responsible "representation and stewardship."[25] Though the Sunnah does record the prophet Muhammad as saying that "God created Adam in His [or his] image",[26] scholars have historically struggled to interpret this because "this kind of intimacy and communion with God and his human creation is unthinkable in Islam."[27] It would be another form of *shirk*.

Mirza Ghulam Ahmad helps explain the reason as to why both Creator and creation are so 'unlike' each

25. Richter, ed., *Comparing the Qur'an and the Bible*, 89.
26. Chawkat Moucarry, *The Prophet & the Messiah* (Downers Grove, IL.: InterVarsity, 2001), 86.
27. Richter, ed., *Comparing the Qur'an and the Bible*, 89.

other by providing a Qur'anic interpretation of man in his *Philosophy of the Teachings of Islam*. He writes that man's being is made up of three inseparable states: physical, moral and spiritual. The first "physical" state, also referred to as the "natural" state, is derived from the surah of *Yusuf*. It is the 'self' that incites man to evil, opposing his "attainment of perfection," and urging him towards undesirable and evil ways (S. 12:54).[28] This "physical" or "natural" state "predominates over the mind of a person," at least until he brings this state under control by means of his own reason and understanding.[29] The second "moral" state of man is rooted in the surah of *al-Qiyamah*, in which the 'self' that reproves "every vice and intemperance" brings about a good state and good morals, where "natural emotions and desires [are] regulated by reason."[30] And the third "spiritual" state of man is derived from the surah of *al-Fajr*, in which the soul of the person is "delivered from all weaknesses," filled with power, and established in a "relationship with God."[31] These three states are not to be perceived as three different 'selves,' but rather as three different states of the one human 'self.' This self being identified with the soul of man, inhabiting a material human body (S. 6:93; 15:29; 17:85; 89:27-28).

What G. Ahmad is attempting to do is make a Qur'anic case for man's totally different nature from

---

28. Mirza Ghulam Ahmad, *The Philosophy of the Teachings of Islam* (Tilford, Surrey: Islam International Publication, 2010), 3-4.

29. Ibid., 4.

30. Ibid., 5.

31. Ibid., 6-7.

his Creator because of his internal struggle. But what is already becoming apparent is the dialectical tension that emerges within Islamic theology, for it is not Allah who brings about control over the first "physical" state, but rather man's own reason and understanding. We can see this in the lack of harmony between the doctrine of Allah and man, where, for example, Salam and Shaikh introduced a basic understanding of *tawhid*'s role in epistemology, but according to Azram, who provides a more comprehensive understanding of Islamic epistemology, "all types of knowledge whether it is Natural Science, Social Science or even Pure Science, should be understood with the aim to establish an Islamic system."[32] In other words, the Islamic system of thought is not already laid out as pre-existing, man in his reason is tasked with carrying this out. He must apply this to nature, he must take what has been revealed, and in applying it, make creation reflect the Islamic worldview. This implies that all knowledge does not solely originate from Allah, but rather that knowledge can exist outside of and independent from himself.

This is evident in Azram's division of knowledge into two branches: revealed knowledge and derived knowledge. In revealed knowledge, there are two components, *fikr* and *dhikr*. The first is a "quest for knowledge," the seeking after the signs of Allah in creation. This knowledge is "rational and attempts to 'reach' God."[33] The latter, however, is a recollection of pre-

---

32. Azram, "Epistemology: An Islamic Perspective", 179.
33. Ibid., 181.

viously attained knowledge through contemplation. When we consult 'derived knowledge' as the second main branch of Islamic epistemology, Azram writes that this knowledge is acquired by our senses, research and deep thinking; the human ability to "conceptualize, acquire, comprehend and search this type of knowledge."[34] So, although the claim is made that all knowledge originates in Allah (S. 49:16), the scholarly work in Islamic epistemology suggests that knowledge can find its origin in something else. How? Because the ultimate starting point for the Muslim mind is not in fact Allah, or the Qur'an, but rather the self-conscious mind which stands as judge to determine what is real, what is knowledgeable, and what is not.

The underlying philosophy of Azram's epistemology is nothing more than rationalism inherited and dressed in Islamic clothing, the belief that "human reason is the final standard of truth,"[35] as with the examination (or reflection) of the order of nature and life, it is the "basic sensible and intellectual capabilities of human beings [which] are appealed to as starting points in our knowledge of God."[36] This is evident in Qur'anic literature (S. 45:3-4),[37] and in Azram's writing, who states that though "divine revelation has always been considered as the ultimate source of knowl-

---

34. Ibid., 181-182.
35. W. Andrew Hoffecker, ed., *Revolutions in Worldview: Understanding the Flow of Western Thought* (Phillipsburg, NJ.: P&R Publishing, 2007), 374.
36. Geisler and Saleeb, *Answering Islam*, 19.
37. See Salam, "Is there an Islamic epistemology? Role of HRD."

edge... it was never the sole."[38] There is, in fact, an unspoken reverence for 'reason' as some abstract existence within nature, which man can somehow tap into. This is also reinforced by scholar Muhammad Amin in his listing of the primary and secondary sources of knowledge in his book *Muslim Epistemology*,[39] and by Ha'iri Yazdi in *The Philosophy of Epistemology in Islamic Philosophy*, who borrows the rationalism of Descartes' "I think, therefore I am" in his theory of *knowledge by presence*.[40] But this abstractual 'reason' is non-existent, it is nothing more than the enlargement of the self,[41] and it persists in Islamic thought largely because of the influence of the Greek philosophers.[42]

In the end, despite the Muslim mind insisting that the god of Islam is their ultimate starting point, it's clear in both the appeals of the Qur'anic text (S. 45:3-4; cf. 51:20-21; 41:53) and the work of Islamic theologians that their ultimate starting point is their 'intellectual self-sufficiency,' by which they work up to a

38. Azram, "Epistemology: An Islamic Perspective", 180.

39. Muhammad Amin, *Muslim Epistemology: An Analytical Appraisal of Islamization of Knowledge* (Pakistan: Educational Reforms Trust Pakistan, 2009), 17.

40. Mehdi Ha'iri Yazdi, *The Principles of Epistemology in Islamic Philosophy* (Albany, NY.: State University of New York Press, 1992), 1-2.

41. H. Evan Runner, *The Relation of the Bible to Learning* (Jordan Station, ON.: Paideia Press, 1982), 97.

42. See, as an example, Al-Kindi, and how Greek philosophy (particularly Aristotle) and its respective terminology influenced Islamic theology and philosophy in Ali El-Konaissi, *Early Muslim Concept of Epistemology* (Belgium: Communication & Cognition, 2003), 15-31.

'rational' acceptance of the Qur'an.[43] But let us grant, for the sake of argument, that man can somehow 'reason' his own way to (the unknowable) Allah. According to G. Ahmad, the latter two states of the human self (the moral and spiritual) are negatively affected by the first "physical" or "natural" state which incites evil, a state which corrupts. In following this line of thought, we must ask just how man's intellect remains unaffected by this corruption? What this implies is that man's attempt to know and predicate reality should be hijacked, reducing him to be much "like the animals," as Ahmad puts it.[44] This would also render him incapable of justifying the intelligibility of reality, for he cannot really know God, nor can he know creation, which is the work of God.

The doctrine of man is just as essential to epistemology as is the doctrine of God, for the beliefs of either doctrine, which are inseparable from each other, result in either the justification or break down of knowledge.[45] And in this case, the Islamic doctrines of God and man results in the latter. It is in analyzing these two fronts that we can identify severe inconsistencies and an incoherence which causes the Islamic worldview to implode. As Robert Reilly writes in *The Closing of the Muslim Mind*, the conclusion is fatal, we are either left with denying "reason's capability of

---

43. Greg L. Bahnsen, *Always Ready: Directions for Defending the Faith*, ed. Robert R. Booth (Nacogdoches, TX.: Covenant Media Press, 2011), 20.

44. G. Ahmad, *The Philosophy of the Teachings of Islam*, 4, 8.

45. Van Til, *Christian Apologetics*, 39-40.

knowing anything," or with dismissing "reality as un-knowable."[46]

5.5 The Christian Worldview

The Christian worldview, however, stands in stark contrast to Islam, and not just on the surface level, such as the differences in theological creeds and practices, but also at its most foundational level. As Van Til puts it, "nothing whatsoever can be known unless God can be and is known... by God we mean the triune, self-sufficient God and his revelation of himself to man and his world."[47] This is the fundamental contention of Christian theism.

The God of Christian theism is not some unknowable abstraction, or a purely isolated singularity. He isn't plural like the gods of polytheistic worship, but rather self-consciously triune, personal, and active. The Father, Son and Holy Spirit are each a personality, not separate from one another outside of the godhead, but rather constituting the "exhaustive personal God."[48] We might refer to the Christian doctrine of the Trinity in two ways, as 'ontological' and 'economical.' When we speak of the ontological Trinity, we refer to the activity of God within Himself. But when we refer to the economical Trinity, we refer to the distinction of persons within the godhead and their work as it concerns creation. Such as, for example, the Father creat-

---

46. Robert R. Reilly, *The Closing of the Muslim Mind: How Intellectual Suicide Created the Modern Islamist Crisis* (Wilmington, Delaware: ISI Books, 2011), Kindle Edition.

47. Van Til, *A Survey of Christian Epistemology*, 103.

48. Van Til, *Christian Apologetics*, 29.

ing and sustaining the universe, the Son bringing about the work of salvation, and the Holy Spirit operating in the subjective work of salvation.[49] In all this, the God of the Bible is self-contained and self-sufficient. He has one kind of being, distinct from creation, eternal, infinite and unchangeable. He is not wholly "other" from creation like the Islamic doctrine of God, for His creation reflects the qualities and attributes of God as much as creation can possibly reflect its Creator. We can see this also in the Christian doctrine of man. However, there is still a clear distinction between Creator and creation, a 'Twoist' worldview (or two-layer of reality), in which the doctrine of God's being is "qualitatively distinct from every other form of being," a defining characteristic solely attributed to the Christian worldview, for all other views are essentially monistic.[50]

Considering, then, that the doctrine of God is inseparable from the whole Christian system of thought, it thus ties into the biblical doctrine of man. Unlike T. Ahmad's Qur'anic interpretation of man, the Bible teaches that man is made up of one self, not composed of multiple states of self, and that he consists of two parts: body and spirit. Both are distinct from each other, the spirit as a substance of its own (as the breath of God), but the union between body and spirit is nonetheless a "life-unity."[51] We also read in Genesis

49. Ibid.

50. Ibid., 31.

51. Geerhardus Vos, *Reformed Dogmatics, Vol. Two: Anthropology*, ed. Richard B. Gaffin, Jr., trans. Richard B. Gaffin, Jr. et al. (Grand Rapids, MI.: Lexham Press, 2012), 1.; Vos uses the term "soul", biblically, however, "spirit" and "soul" are used

1 that man was created in God's image, both Adam and Eve. This sets them apart from the rest of creation, for though they remain 'creaturely' as creations, they are the only creatures who bear God's image.[52] This essentially means that man resembles God in everyway that a creature can be like God, that is, he is a personality, he resembles God's moral attributes, he was created with "true knowledge, true righteousness, and true holiness" (Cf. Col. 3:10; Eph. 4:24).[53] We might say it this way, if God's nature were a stamp, our original nature would be the impression made by the stamp.[54] Of course, to be created in God's image means more than that man is spirit, and possesses some understanding, will, etc.; it means that, above all, he is "disposed for communion with God, that all the capacities of his soul can act in a way that corresponds to their destiny only if they rest in God."[55] Mankind was created as a relational being, to worship God in the totality of his nature, both individually and collectively. This is the chief end for human existence, to glorify God in the fulfillment of his divine purposes as man exercises dominion over the rest of creation.[56]

It is in surveying the Christian doctrines of God and man that we understand that God has self-con-

---

interchangeably. The Greek concept of the "soul" is not to be understood as a *biblical* concept.

52. Ibid., 12.
53. Van Til, *Christian Apologetics*, 40.
54. Vos, *Reformed Dogmatics, Vol. Two*, 14.
55. Ibid., 13.
56. Millard J. Erickson, *Christian Theology*, Third ed. (Grand Rapids, MI.: Baker Academic, 2013), 436, 470.

tained being, that is, He is self-sufficient, while man has created, or derivative being. In the same manner, God has self-contained knowledge, that is, immediate and self-referential, while man has derivative knowledge. In simpler terms, man's being and knowledge are derived from his Creator.[57] This is better clarified by the Christian scholar Greg L. Bahnsen, who writes that "God's knowledge is primary, and whatever man is to know can only be based upon a reception of what God has originally and ultimately known."[58] This concept, however, of man's being and knowledge being derivative, is impossible to fathom in Islamic theology, it inevitably leads to *shirk*, though it is fundamental to Christian theology.

Whereas in Islam, an impersonal, non-relational being cannot create personal, relational beings, Christian theism explains that the true personal, relational triune God can, and did, create personal, relational beings. It is the qualities of the biblical God that, as theologian Millard J. Erickson writes, "reflected in human beings, make worship, personal interactions, and work possible."[59]

If this is true then, that man was created in God's image with true knowledge, true righteousness, and true holiness, why is there so sharp a disagreement between human persons as it concerns epistemology, predication, morality and ethics? The present portrait of humanity, after all, is not one of true knowledge,

---

57. Van Til, *Christian Apologetics*, 31.
58. Bahnsen, *Always Ready*, 19.
59. Erickson, *Christian Theology*, 471.

nor of righteousness or holiness, but rather of a creation whose image of God has been effaced. The answer lies in the historical garden of Eden, original sin. God had created man with a moral compass, he had transmitted His ordinances, His law, into man's being. So long as man lived in obedience to God's law, he was living in accord with his own true nature.[60] But in disobeying God by eating from the forbidden tree, it was not merely the act, but the intention behind the act which communicated the sinful spirit that would follow thereafter. It was an attempt to do away with God altogether, in every respect, as he sought for his own "ideals of truth, goodness and beauty somewhere beyond God, either directly within himself or indirectly within the universe about him."[61] This is exactly what we see in the dialectical tension within the Muslim mind, the assertion of Allah as their ultimate starting point while their finite consciousness serves as the real locus of authority.

Sin has ravaged the totality of man's being, it has caused a "radical reversal" as Vos puts it, because as he has fallen from that which he was originally disposed, diverting him from his true nature and destiny, his resulting disorganization means spiritual death, a "process of dissolution."[62] This means that in the falling away from original righteousness, what takes its place as the 'natural' state of man is unrighteousness. He thus cannot help but operate in unrighteousness, and

60. Van Til, *Christian Apologetics*, 42.
61. Ibid.
62. Vos, *Reformed Dogmatics, Vol. Two*, 14.

this extends to his intellectual capacities as well, what theologians refer to as the *noetic* effects of sin.[63] The Bible teaches that man, in his sin nature, suppresses the truth (Rom. 1:18), meaning that the true knowledge which man was originally created with has not been lost, but rather, is suppressed as a form of moral rebellion. As a late commentator had written, "Everything in them and around them testifies to God, but they reject the testimony of all creation, and of their own being... to deny this revelation is for man to deny his own being."[64] It is, therefore, characteristic of the unbelieving mind to be willfully ignorant of the God of Christian theism, even though their own antithetical worldviews are unsustainable and futile, unable to predicate reality and to provide the pre-conditions of intelligibility.

5.6 The Verdict

This understanding of the noetic effects of sin thus provides light and clarity as to how we can understand the difference between the Muslim and Christian mind, for both the Muslim and the Christian will agree with each other about certain "facts" about reality, such as, for example, our self-consciousness; but this is merely our immediate starting point. The real difference between the Muslim and the Christian is whether they *truly* know the facts, that is, can they make sense of the facts from their respective presuppositions, from their ultimate starting point. And from the outset, the

---

63. Ibid., 26.

64. Rousas J. Rushdoony, *Romans & Galatians* (Vallecito, CA.: Ross House Books, 1997), 13.

Muslim cannot help but fail to make sense of the facts from the Islamic system of thought, because he is attempting to interpret the facts as independent, or separated, from Christian theism. He cannot *truly* know the facts, the underlying philosophy of the facts, because he presupposes a different god than that of the Christian Scriptures, when the facts of reality are God's facts, not Allah's.[65]

What then is the ultimate starting point for the Christian mind, and by this we mean a regenerated mind that is faithful to the Christian Scriptures? It is the triune God of Christian theism, who is known to us not only by our nature as being created in God's image, and by the natural revelation all around us, but through His revealed word. As Bahnsen explains, "the Christian presupposes the truthful word of God as his standard of truth and direction."[66] It is only by presupposing the truth of Christian theism that we can have *true* knowledge of anything, it is the promised result of reflecting God's primary knowledge. To actually do this, however, involves renouncing our own intellectual self-sufficiency, the belief that we can somehow attain knowledge independently of God's standards and directions.[67] But this implies a change that goes far deeper than the intellect, it constitutes a revolutionary change of our human nature, from sinful and corrupted to restored and renewed, a work that can only be carried out in Christ Jesus (Col. 3:10-12).

---

65. Van Til, *A Survey of Christian Epistemology*, 114-115.

66. Bahnsen, *Always Ready*, 19.

67. Ibid., 20.

When it comes down to which of the two world-views provides the pre-conditions of intelligibility, we are essentially asking which worldview makes human experience intelligible. The answer is the same as with any other worldview comparison, Christianity alone. It is, after all, the *only* reasonable worldview. As Van Til succinctly wrote:

> Now in fact, I feel that the whole of history and civili-zation would be unintelligible to me if it were not for my belief in God. So true is this, that I propose to argue that unless God is back of everything, you cannot find meaning in anything.[68]

No epistemic foundation can rival that of the Christian worldview, not even a counterfeit like Islam, for without Christian theism, all of reality would cease to be intelligible.

---

68. Cornelius Van Til, *Why I Believe in God* (Philadelphia: Com-mittee on Christian Education of the Orthodox Presbyteri-an Church, n.d.), 3.

Scripture Index

Person Index

Subject Index

About the Author

Steven R. Martins is the founding director of the Cántaro Institute and founding pastor of Sevilla Chapel in St. Catharines, Ontario, Canada. A second-generation Canadian, Steven is of Ibero-American parentage and has worked in the fields of missional apologetics and church leadership for eight years. He has spoken at numerous conferences, churches, and University student events, from York University, Toronto, to the University of West Indies in Port of Spain, Trinidad, and the national Universities of Costa Rica (UNCR and UNC), and the Evangelical University of El Salvador. He has also contributed articles to Coalición por el Evangelio (TGC in Spanish) and the *Siglo XXI* journal of Editorial CLIR.

Steven holds a Master's degree *summa cum laude* in Theological Studies with a focus on Christian apologetics from Veritas International University (Santa Ana, CA., USA) and a Bachelor of Human Resource Management from York University (Toronto, ON., Canada). Steven has served on the executive board for Answers in Genesis Canada, and has served in the past with the Ezra Institute for Contemporary Christianity (EICC) as a staff apologist, writer and director of ministry development and advancement (DMDA) for four years. He has also served pastorally at Harbour Fellowship Church in St. Catharines. Steven is married to Cindy and lives in Jordan Station, Ontario, with their children Matthias and Timothy.

CPSIA information can be obtained
at www.ICGtesting.com
Printed in the USA
LVHW081145211020
669386LV00005B/679